BUSTER KEATON

In the same
INTERNATIONAL FILM GUIDE SERIES
edited by Peter Cowie

BUSTER KEATON

by J.-P. LEBEL
translated by P. D. STOVIN

A. ZWEMMER LIMITED, LONDON
A. S. BARNES & CO., NEW YORK

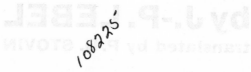

108225

ENGLISH EDITION FIRST PUBLISHED 1967

and prepared by the Tantivy Press in association with A. Zwemmer Ltd. and A. S. Barnes & Co. Inc.

Contents

Contents

"To understand a work, one should not criticise intentions but instead discover its sense in the very forms it invents."

Jean Hilar

BUSTER Keaton, christened Joseph Francis Keaton, was born on his parents' farm in Pickway, Kansas, on October 4, 1895. His parents were of Scottish and Irish descent.

"I first walked the boards in 1899, at the age of three. My father and mother put me into their vaudeville act, which had a lot of acrobatics in it. You might say I was brought up on the stage."[1]

"Wearing a wig and enormous sideburns, he leaped and tumbled with his father, who dragged him on stage and walked all over him. The great Harry Houdini gave young Keaton his nickname after having particularly admired the way the little acrobat fell flat on his back down a flight of stairs."[2]

" . . . In 1917, our act, 'The Three Keatons', came to an end. One fine morning my father blew up in the theatre manager's office and chased him out into the street. Our engagements were cancelled — we were left high and dry. I sent my parents back home and took the train to New York. I met Fatty Arbuckle on 46th Street and he asked me to work with him for the movies. The idea appealed to me and I went with him to the studio where I met his producer, Joseph Schenck. I did a few turns for Schenck and he offered me 40 dollars a week. So I went back to the Schubert Revue and announced that I'd been made an offer to play in films and told them to tear up my contract . . . and that's how I got my start in the movies."

"*You gave up a contract for 750 dollars a week merely for the*

[1] A Quatre Temps, *Cahiers du Cinéma*, no. 130, April 1962.

[2] *Cahiers du Cinéma*, no. 86, August 1958.

11

pleasure of making films?"

"Money never interested me very much and besides, I wanted to see what it was like . . ."[3]

He made several shorts with Arbuckle which the latter directed for Joseph Schenck.

In 1918 the war interrupted this film series. Keaton spent several months in France with the 159th infantry regiment of the 40th division. He remained in France until the armistice.

Back in the United States he made several more films with Arbuckle, and then, together with Eddie Cline and still for Joseph Schenck, he played in and directed two-reelers, first for Metro Pictures Corporation, then for First National.

Meanwhile, in 1920, he made his first real appearance in *The Saphead*, a filmed adaptation of a stage hit by Bronson Howard, *The Henrietta*, which Douglas Fairbanks had starred in on Broadway.

In 1923 Keaton went to M-G-M where he made a series of full-length films.

In 1926 he left M-G-M for United Artists, where he made his last four silent films.

In 1929 he made his first "talkie", *The Spite Marriage*. This was the last film that Joseph Schenck produced for him.

Buster Keaton's decline began with the talkie.

From 1929 to 1933 he made a series of feature length talkies, once again at M-G-M. These films had neither the quality nor the success of his silent films.

In 1934 he decided to try his luck in Europe. The two films he made there were failures. Discouraged, he returned to the States

[3] *Cahiers du Cinéma*, no. 86, August 1958.

12

where he began a long struggle against encroaching neurasthenia.

From 1934 to 1937, under the direction of Charles Lamont, he made a series of shorts for First National and the "Educational Film Corporation". These films were comparatively worthless.

In 1937 he spent a year in a psychiatric clinic.

In 1938 he was back at M-G-M, this time as gag-man (particularly for Red Skelton), assistant director and scenario writer.

From 1939 to 1945 he played occasional small roles in different comedies.

In 1946 he tried his luck in Mexico: Jaime Salvador's *El Moderno Barba Azul*.

Keaton was then reduced to sporadic appearances, in, among others, Billy Wilder's *Sunset Boulevard*, where he played himself, Chaplin's *Limelight* where he, at the piano, accompanied Chaplin on the violin, Michael Anderson's *Around the World in 80 Days*, and Stanley Kramer's *It's a Mad, Mad, Mad, Mad World*.

He made tours in European circuses. Twice, in 1952 and again in 1954, he was to be applauded in Paris at the Cirque Médrano. He appeared on English television.

In 1957 he supervised the film on his life produced for Paramount by Sidney Sheldon.

In 1962, following the revival of *The General*, there was talk of re-editing some of Keaton's other films. This was to begin in Germany, and the films are *Steamboat Bill Junior*, *The Navigator* and *Our Hospitality*.

From Thursday February 23 to Monday March 5, 1962, on the occasion of Buster Keaton's passing through Paris, the French Cinémathèque organised a retrospective season of all his silent feature films and most of his shorts; we shall never be able to express adequately our gratitude for this season.

1. The Great Stone Face

> "He who says impassivity does not say insensitivity, and he who does not say insensitivity does not say sadness, distress, despair."
> Lee Rockoy

FOR a long time Buster Keaton's impassivity was considered not only his dominant physical trait but his dominant comic trait as well. It is that which inspired all the idiotic epithets about him, such as "The man who never smiles",[1] or the nickname, "Firgo", given him in France. This stupid name, capable at best of calling to mind a brand of refrigerator, reduces Keaton's face to a slab of refrigerated meat, and is utterly incapable of suggesting the ardent impenetrability, the frozen fire, the mute and diamond fervour of this face so calm and supreme with, behind the burnt sockets, its two bright flaming eyes.

People tried to see in Keaton's impassivity a trick, to consider it the unique accessory, the one mildly humorous attraction to be found in a worn-out clown otherwise lacking in imagination. They reduced his impassivity to a kind of insensitivity, and applied the well-worn term "phlegmatic" to his comic style. They felt obliged to reduce his opaque mask to something they themselves could understand, and not accept it for the disquieting thing it was: a face turned in upon itself, concentrating upon itself with a prolonged and unbearable determination.

This incomprehension was primarily a product of the times. At

---

[1] An appellation indicative of that Hollywood publicity which accorded Erich von Stroheim the epithet "The man you love to hate". The two men are brothers within this incomprehension, for both the pantomime genius and the maker of *Greed* saw themselves systematically divested of all possibility of expressing themselves by those merchants of mindlessness who consigned them, with artificial glory, to third-rate scripts and false and insincere praise.

15

a moment when acting styles[2] were based on an excess of mimicry and the cinema was considered an art of facial pantomime on white canvas, the "enlightened", in the spirit of the times, could only conceive of this expressive impenetrability as being something anti-artistic, something incapable of expressing the sacrosanct human emotions, and thus as a rather coarse and schematic comic artifice. It was all, therefore, just one more proof that comedy was good for the people, a vulgar cinematic form poles away from the sublime, not reflecting that observational perspicaciousness of the little tics of "human nature" that alone gives comedy a certain dimension.

From Fatty Arbuckle's gross grimaces to the perfection of Chaplin's wonderful facial mobility, comedy was defined for the public as a sort of facial gymnastics going merely from the vulgar to the subtle. In this context it is hardly surprising that Keaton's mask appear an incomprehensible anomaly, a riddle considerably more difficult to unravel than that of the Sphinx. Nor was it surprising that one should hasten to imprison Keaton in his oddness, to transform his anomaly into a label. What made him different would serve to identify him, to catalogue him. Buster Keaton became "the man who never smiles". This reassuring and, in some ways, controlled appellation, became his title to glory.

Later, of course,[3] when cinematic sensitivity and acting styles had matured, some began to feel that Keaton's expressive facial discretion, far from being a sign of insensitivity, was really a sign of hyper-sensitivity. This came at a time when the public had developed a frenzied admiration for "under-acting", and when all actors playing "soberly" were praised for their great subtlety. Now, with

[2] Not merely comic styles but also, and especially, tragic ones.

[3] And even sooner, among the more clairvoyant.

16

Above: THE THREE AGES.   *Below: with Fatty Arbuckle.*

the aid of the "Kuleshov effect", Keaton's mask entered the domain of "profound emotion". Of course, no sooner does one talk of profound emotion than one has recourse to a whole scale of fixed and catalogued emotions that can be applied once and for all. Keaton immediately began to represent the tragedy of the human condition[4], and, on the screen, his face was soon painted with sweeping strokes of distress and despair.

One thing remains constant: whether one makes of Keaton's mask a trick and the mark of comic superficiality or one makes of it the image of tragic human destiny; whether one sees in him mere dead indifference or one sees the ridiculous symbol of human pathos, there is no getting around the expressive fixity of his face. His impassivity is sanctioned by being reduced to the concentrated expression of a single emotion turned upon itself. His head becomes a head reduced, forever petrified in an unchanging expression.

We are in the presence of a purely static definition of Keaton's expressiveness.

Attempting to explain the comic virtues of his facial rigidity, Keaton offers the following explanation, drawn from his music-hall observations: "The greater a comic's indifference, the more astonished he seems by the public's laughter", the greater that burst of laughter will be.[5]

Such a declaration would tend to give weight to the idea that his impassivity is a "comic trick". But of course it is! No one would dream of denying that Keaton played on his impassivity; but to reduce his comic style uniquely to that is something we refuse to do.

---

[4] This being the highest criterion of the Catholic Review Board, it is incontestably the most profound insight that has been arrived at to date.

[5] Buster Keaton: "Le Métier de faire rire", in *Anthologie du Cinéma* by Marcel Lapierre, Paris 1946, p. 355.

First of all, let us note that the technique Keaton speaks of is first and foremost a music-hall technique, conceived on a stage where the comic has an audience at his feet and can use the reactions of the audience as a guide in his act; the problem in the cinema is another one entirely; the comic has no audience, no laughter or lack of it to guide him; he must instead submit all he does to a sort of internal logic linked to the world of the particular film and to that world only. The style of the first cinema comics who winked at the audience as Fatty Arbuckle did, for example, "so that," as Keaton said, "the audience laughed *with* him whereas the audience laughs *at* me"[6], this differentiation of styles is still possible — in this form — so long as the cinema comic is still only the pure and simple transcription of the theatre comic. But as soon as the film takes on its own particular structure and creates its own particular world of interacting characters, as soon as the "objective illusion" of the cinema comes into play, this differentiation can no longer exist, or, more precisely, can exist only in the Keaton kind of comedy as opposed to the Arbuckle kind. The film itself, the world of the film, becomes laughable. And thus one laughs *at* Keaton and *at* the film; but this laughter is no longer linked to facial impassivity, to the absence of reactions and to the character's indifference *within* the film's reality.

Then too, this facial impassivity considered as an absence of reactions to the comic situation would be convincing if it applied to the whole of Keaton's person. However, if his mask belies no emotion, his body, on the contrary, constantly manifests an imme-diate reaction, and indeed almost never comes to rest. Keaton's style of comedy is therefore not essentially phlegmatic, and one must seek the reason for his facial impenetrability elsewhere.

*　　　*　　　*

It is necessary to state first of all that Keaton's impassivity *is not a voluntary decision on his part*. This therefore excludes the possibility of its being a "comic trick" on which his whole technique is based, providing the publicity men with the easy catch-phrase, "the man who never laughs"[7] which would tend to make one think the contrary.

What's more, no declaration from Keaton to this effect is required to realise this, since Keaton never tried to introduce a sense of complicity between the public and himself. His impassivity can therefore be linked neither to the idea of the "English euphemism", nor to that style of comedy which consists of acting "as if nothing funny had happened" and simulating astonishment at the public's laughter. In a word, Keaton's impassivity *is not an affectation*.

Keaton himself declares: "When I began to have this reputation for impassivity, we went through my films to see if it was really true that I never smiled; I wasn't even aware of it myself."[8]

If, then, Keaton's impassivity is not an affectation, it is part of his normal behaviour. It is an aspect of his personality, and does not try to be anything else. As we shall see, the same holds for all the other aspects of his personality. Keaton is not trying to prove something: he is attitude, he is gesture, he is action. That's all, and the rest is literature.

And Keaton himself, in a statement made elsewhere, gives us

[7] Or, "the man who never smiles" — the original catch-phrase is uncertain.

[8] "Interview with Buster Keaton" by Christopher Bishop. Translated into French by J. P. Coursodon in *Cinéma 60*, no. 49, August-September 1960.

the key to the problem; and his statement, in its marvellous simplicity, not only gives us the key to his impassivity, but to his whole personality as well: "I concentrated on what I was doing."[9]

He "concentrated" and the word "concentration" brings together all the characteristics that can be attributed to the Keaton mask:

— Firstly a prodigious *attention* to the world.

— Then, a *reflective* comic style.

— Lastly, a *tense and concentrated energy*, an ardour crystallised in the seemingly impassive face and, particularly, in the eyes.

Far from shutting him off from the world, his face reflects a great openness towards all things and all situations. But this openness is not impulsiveness; it is reflection and concentration. Nothing astonishes Buster Keaton because he considers all with the same undivided attention: he has no prejudices.

In *Cops*, as Keaton drives along in his battered old car, he suddenly finds himself in the midst of a policemen's parade; remarking the crowd's enthusiasm for the parade, he naturally assumes that the cheers are meant for him and, impassive, waves first to the left, then to the right. His action is not meant to be ostentatious; it is merely one of the most elementary good manners.

In *Cops*, too, Keaton fearlessly and naturally lights his cigarette from the burning fuse of the bomb that an anarchist has just thrown on to the seat beside him. This gesture is not one of provocation — Keaton is not an anarchist, but at the same time he is not an anti-anarchist; this bomb, with its burning fuse, is precisely what he needs to light his cigarette. And he uses it for that, nothing more.

---

[9] "A Meeting with Buster Keaton" by John Schmitz. Translated into French by J. P. Coursodon in *Cahiers du Cinéma*, no. 86, August 1958.

When he does panic it is only because the panic of the crowd becomes contagious. From the crowd's cries he realizes that something is amiss and he throws the bomb away (and suffers the gravest consequences for this action: for this attention ever on the alert; for this openness which makes him unable to refuse whatever offers itself, he will pay with his life).

The proof of Keaton's lack of ostentation is that he very seldom uses his impassivity for the sake of a gag; he never deliberately tries to make it funny by some wild and intrepid action. In *The General*, however, we do find a pure illustration[10] of the reflective side of Keaton's comic style which does reside in his impassivity, an illustration which offers us a perfect example of his determined, deft and deaf-eared way of proceeding. The scene takes place at dawn, after a particularly fatiguing night, when, in a stance of truly heroic proportions (such as Lancelot alone, lost in the forest with Guinevere, would have any right to assume), Johnny Gray suddenly becomes aware of the unpleasant situation he and Annabelle are in, and at the same time perceives the Northern troops in the act of loading a train. What happens then is a brilliant example of the Kuleshov effect which is both an example of pure cinema directing and of the comic "milking" of Keaton's impassivity. There is first a shot of the Northern troops, then a shot of Keaton, a living model of concentration and reflection in action; then a shot of the girl, and another shot of Keaton, meditating. In the following shots — passing from the idea to the act — Keaton knocks out a Northern sol-

---

[10] By this I do not mean to imply that Keaton's impassivity has nothing to do with his comic style. Far from it. But more often than not his impassivity is not the *source* of the gag. This so-called impassivity is part of the person who is Buster Keaton, a fundamental part of his attitude towards the world, and therefore a constant which only rarely acquires — and then in terms of particular situations, most often when Keaton himself is not in action, which is seldom — a uniquely determining function in the birth of the gag.

dier, makes off with his sack, empties it of the boots with which it's filled, and puts "tender, touching Annabelle" inside.

But if Keaton's impassivity is a mark of reflection, this is not necessarily to say that he always finds the solution to every problem. Keaton, being human, has his moments of astonished irresolution and sudden fright. The marble fearlessness of his face then becomes a sign of that last hold on equilibrium with which his mind, striving to understand (a despairing attempt, tension stretched to snapping point), still restrains his body before it succumbs at last to helter-skelter flight, a final solution when none more efficacious is forthcoming. Thus, in *The Navigator*, when presented with the monstrous sight of that terrifying sailor — the werewolf of the seas — dangling before his porthole, Keaton's facial fixedness is nothing more nor less than a tense, panic-controlling effort to understand, an instant held in time, a kind of dizziness preceding the desperate run for his life, the panicked terror of his body which no longer obeys his will[11] and which, faced with his mind's failure to grapple with the problem, once again finds the most efficacious solution in flight.

But it is already obvious that one cannot study "the impassivity" of Keaton's face by itself, one thing leads to another, the face leads to action and action leads to the body.

But before we finish with this characterisation of Keaton's "impassivity" as concentration, let us examine a passage from *The General* in which the three aspects of this concentration all come into play.

Johnny Gray has gone in pursuit of the Northerners who have kidnapped his "General" and, with it, his fiancée. The Northerners have uncoupled the General's guard's van in order to block the

---

[11] Or which, rather, divines its intentions before they have been formulated.

track. Keaton avails himself of a branchline to get rid of the van; he shunts it on to the side-track, re-adjusts the points, gets back in his locomotive and takes off again (all this in his inimitable race rhythm, imperially and rapidly, without panic or haste). But we soon discover that this track — a side-track but a vicious one — returns upon itself after a slight curve. Keaton crams the boiler full in order to take up the chase and make up for lost time. Intent on its goal, his face, seen in close-up when he returns to the driver's seat to survey the track, is all *concentrated energy*. Now he discovers the van to be in front of him again. And as he does so his face changes imperceptibly, his eyes widen slightly and his pseudo-impassivity turns from *tense energy* to *intense reflection*. Still calm, he tries to understand, and turns to make sure that the van isn't really behind him. While his head is turned the van is de-railed, taking with it a log that the Northerners, as logically malevolent towards him as ever, had laid on the track as another obstacle. Turning back to the track ahead of him, impassive as ever but beginning to understand, Keaton now finds that the van has totally disappeared. He doesn't flinch, but we nevertheless notice a sort of imperceptible puckering. He doesn't panic, but, intrepid, once again gives himself over to intense meditation. Some verifications first: perhaps his eyes deceived him. He blinks, but no, it's neither a mirage nor a dream, the van has definitely disappeared. He looks behind him once again and, the verifications done, returns to his driver's seat, all tense energy and attention concentrated on the chase.

Let us note in passing that Keaton's kind of reflection is not at all a purely speculative one; it exists only in terms of his action, together with the careful attention he accords to the world around him, and the manifestation of his energy. He may not understand exactly how the van disappeared from the track but he doesn't waste his time in vain imaginings. What interests him, and what gives him food for reflection, is the pure and simple fact that the van has disappeared — and this fact conditions his action. Whenever Keaton reflects, he does so for an active purpose.

We can see from the above example that Keaton's "impassivity" is merely a pseudo-impassivity, and that, no matter how imperceptible they may seem to be, changes do take place on his physiognomy.

If Keaton's face attains a sort of classic perfection, in its stripping down and its almost total nudity, that is because it harbours within it an energy and an expressive richness concentrated to the point of rarefaction. The slightest change of expression, the slightest movement of his physiognomy — i.e. the smallest *efficacious* expenditure of energy on his face — is alive with an extraordinary amount of *accumulated latent energy*. Keaton's face might be compared to a fissionable atom: extraordinary power hides in the smallest possible particle, pushing matter towards disintegration. The proof of Keaton's intensity is in his flaming eyes.

One begins to have a certain idea of the force stored up behind this tense, smooth mask when Keaton suddenly lets himself go: his body explodes in a fantastic eruption of energy as, at the same time, he give himself up to a visual pantomime of the most dazzling expressiveness imaginable. Suddenly he becomes all head and legs. His head seems to act as a reservoir for his body, storing up all the energy and expressiveness from which his body draws its strength for its marvellous dances and deeds.

The power of the eruption gives an idea of the degree of concentration.

And thus it seems that the famous Keaton "impassivity" is but a legend — at least as generally described. Besides which, there are no grounds for the belief that he offers only an immovable, unchanging mask to the world. One need only recall the scene in *The General* where, hiding beneath the table in the Northern headquarters and soaked to the skin, Keaton represses a desire to sneeze with dexterity and elegance by pressing a finger against his nostril. Here his face does pucker and his aspect change.

What's more, the living and changing presence of his eyes belies that rigidity attributed to his face. Keaton's eyes are the furthest points of his attention to reality, the watch-tower of his face; they are the living manifestation of his facial potential.

Thus, in the famous passage in *Our Hospitality* where Keaton is at table with his enemies in an atmosphere of mutual suspicion and distrust, his whole life can be seen in his eyes: ever on the alert, amazingly mobile, they never pause in their activity, surveying their enemies, evaluating the danger, weighing every detail and preparing for all eventualities.

In the abovementioned scene from *The General*, when Keaton, beneath the table in the Union Headquarters, looks through a hole that an officer's cigar has burnt in the tablecloth, his eye turns in the hole as he tries to explore all he can of the field. And it is as if the incandescent tip of the cigar, with its radiant intensity, had found its way into his socket and remained there, glowing. All Keaton's being seems concentrated in this single eye.

It is clear from what we have written that Keaton's emotions and feelings, manifesting themselves on the seemingly immobile lake of his face, cannot be analysed statically or limited to that. They must be studied in the light of his comportment in the world; a study of his face leads to a study of his bodily mechanics; from facial "impassivity" we move to bodily "gesture", to the etching of his body in space.

But before going any further, we should like, in the wake of so many others, to say a word about Buster Keaton's beauty, about the beauty of this Sioux-like profile, with its thick fleece of hair on the nape; about the beauty of this grave face, full of fervour, nobility, energy and intelligence; about the beauty of the nudity and the simple classic perfection of this face reduced to its simplest and most intense expression.

That this beauty, for us, can be explained in terms of concentration of expression, attention, energy, tenacity, fervour, reflection, certitude going beyond obstacles and despair (although we can also often read therein of infinite disappointment and endless worry — both always overcome) does not hinder us from simply finding Buster Keaton's face both beautiful and touching.

And so we add our voice to those who defend Keaton against those (of whom here are still too many) who see nothing but muteness and inexpressiveness in this admirable figure of a man.

2. The Perfect Geometry

AS Jean-Marc Leuwen has very rightly pointed out[1], Buster Keaton had no special quirks. "Keaton is not a 'character'", writes Leuwen. Which is not to say that he lacks a behavioural coherence or fails to create a special world in which his comic character exists. But Keaton never felt obliged to add extraneous artificial elements to his normal appearance. In a word, the character created by Keaton is not a 'character role' . . . "(He) refuses to disguise himself. He is his own hero, like Cocteau in *Le Testament d'Orphée*, wearing neither make-up, false paunch, stereotyped smile, moustache nor spectacles".

As for clothing, if Keaton does not wear one particular identifying garment throughout his films, and unmistakable elegance shines through everything he puts on, an elegance discreet and fragile but, at the same time, constant and sure. For him it is a show of nobility to the world, a lofty protest.

In dinner-jacket and top hat, in sweater and cap, in a grey suit with its flat little hat or in the overalls of a railway engineer, his humble and steadfast profile ever imposes its gracious form on the world around him.

And yet, though Keaton did not create himself a "character" with the aid of sartorial accessories, certain items do crop up over and over again in his films. And thus we have the little flat-brimmed hat which — apart from its pathetic ridiculousness – extends and effaces the obstinacy of his brow and accentuates, in profile, the pull of his head towards the front. All caps become him, especially when he turns their peaks to the back.

---

[1] J. M. Leuwen, "Buster Keaton", *Cinéma 60*, no. 49, August-September 1960.

That Keaton's clothing drapes him with an inimitable elegance, and that he often is dressed to the nines, has nothing to do with any desire on his part to show off. With him the dress-coat and dinner-jacket are not so much signs of a snobbishness and class affectation (as regards both social status and physical appearance) as they are of a simple and natural elegance. Keaton does not "bring out" clothing so much as clothing "brings out" Keaton. Clothing exists to reveal the man. Besides which, Keaton's clothing often serves as mourning dress. I am thinking of that scene in *Battling Butler* when, immediately before his scheduled combat with the "Alabama Murderer", Keaton, a little impostor with no idea how to box, comes into the changing-room in evening-dress, white gloves and top hat. His pathetic appearance of mourning here is his dignity's final protest, his will's last refusal to admit defeat, his whole being's determination to face his adversary with courage even when he knows he will be beaten; the mute, fragile and certain affirmation of his existence in space — as if he knew, in all modesty, that his beauty, gravity and dignity make him invulnerable.

Keaton does not so much fit into his clothing as his clothing fits over him. And this becomes especially clear when he takes it off.[2]

Of all the great cinema comics, Keaton alone comes off to advantage when clad only in shorts.

In a bathing costume on a beach, without his glasses, Harold Lloyd is nothing but another middle-class American playboy. Harry Langdon, nude, would be monstrously babyish, indecent perhaps. Laurel and Hardy have often been seen in pants (impossible to imagine Keaton thus clad), as, for that matter, they have

---

[2] In the following passage the word "nudity" will not merely mean simple physical nakedness; one is "nude" in my sense of the word when clothing no longer hides the body's natural poise.

also been seen in nappies, but rarely nude. Or, more precisely, their more or less relative nakedness is turned into a "comic situation", and a generally degrading one. Nudity for them is not a suit of clothing. The few scenes of full comic nudity in the cinema — like Gabriello's, for instance, in Abel Gance's *La Tour de Nesle* — are only comic insofar as they are degrading, and their comic value stems from the fact that they place their characters in embarrassing situations. The systematic and frenzied use of the nightshirt and long underdrawers to comic ends are directly related to vaudeville and bedroom farce.

The Marx Brothers' magnificent aggressiveness would be seriously compromised were they to undress (unless the act of undressing itself were intended to be an act of provocation).

One has rarely seen Chaplin nude. Oh, from time to time, cane in hand and bowler on his head, he *has* appeared shirtless, with only a pair of suspenders over his naked chest. But Chaplin wears *trousers*, and baggy ones at that; a bare-legged Chaplin is inconceivable. True, in his early years, he was sometimes to be seen sporting a pair of vintage 1900 bathing drawers, but in such a get-up Chaplin the tramp did not really exist anymore, unless one might say that he existed through his bowler and walking stick. But with his walking-stick, Chaplin isn't really naked. But Chaplin is a genius and can divest himself if he chooses of the tramp's outfittings which made his glory without imprisoning him; and King Shadow in his dressing gown is as beautiful as Chaplin dancing in the street.

Keaton alone wears his nudity with elegance and grace. Keaton nude is still Keaton. Suffering countless rebuffs, performing daring acrobatic and prehistoric feats in scenes which necessitate nudity (*College, Battling Butler, The Three Ages*), the vibrations and modulations of Keaton's form remain constant and constantly pleasing.

For Keaton's form fits his body to perfection. Clothed, the harmony of his appearance is the harmony of his muscular poise and his body's spare grace.

Buster Keaton's films provide the meeting ground for man and the world, and show this meeting in a comedy and an ethic of action; encountering the world on physical and spatial terms, man appears, as he has appeared throughout history, in his most naked, elemental form. In his struggle against the universe, he begins by merely trying to survive; later he affirms his existence in space.

If, then, Keaton's body is the *expression* of his personality, if his form alone already incarnates and concentrates all his virtualities, these virtualities explode into being when his body which, even at rest[3], is budding dynamism (straining towards movement, restraining movement), finally lets go and gives us a real taste of what Keaton, dynamism burst into flower, can do.

"If what Chaplin retained of the Mack Sennett heritage was the indefatigable *agitato* of the first burlesque comedies, what Keaton retained was precisely its acrobatic and athletic qualities"[4].

Buster Keaton, reared on the stage — and in that he differs little from most other American vaudeville comedians who also picked up much of what they knew as children, getting acrobatic training in circuses or music halls (or, more often than not, in both) — is an authentic acrobat. He himself has this to say about his early training: "The kid growing up in the wings imitates all he sees; if a tightrope walker comes one week, he'll try walking a taut cord when nobody's looking; if a juggler comes, he'll try juggling; he'll try tumbling, he'll try everything . . . I even imitated Harry Houdini"[5].

[3] Something so rare that the statement is almost self-contradictory.

[4] André Martin: "Le Mécano de la Pantomime", *Cahiers du Cinéma*, no. 86, August, 1958, p. 21.

[5] "Interview with Buster Keaton" by Christopher Bishop, *Cinéma 60*, August-September 1960, p. 67-68.

A full list of the acrobatic exploits performed by Keaton in his films would be impossible. It is common knowledge that only once in his career did he use a stand-in, and then for a feat which required absolute technical mastery. The film was *College*. Keaton hired Lee Barnes, the champion Olympic pole-jumper, to leap from a second-storey window to the spot where his love was suffering in the hands of the "villain".

In *Paleface* Keaton dived into a net from a suspension-bridge 75 feet high. But here is André Martin on Keaton's feats: "In *Hard Luck* he had to leap from a 45 foot diving-board, miss the pool and fall on to the "marble" paving stones. These stones were made of paper and placed on a thick layer of sawdust. He seriously injured his head and shoulder while "playing" this scene.

"In *Sherlock Junior* he had to find himself seated on the handle-bars of a speeding motorcycle without realising that he'd lost the driver. He roared down the most crowded street of a city, cut a cord that two teams of athletes were contending for, received shovelfuls of earth in the face, one after the other, as they were thrown with perfect synchronization by a team of entrenched roaddiggers, bore down on a fallen tree which blocked the road and which a fortuitous explosion halved at the last moment, crashed into a car, was thrown into the air, flew through a cabin window, knocked the traitor through the cabin wall with his feet and thereby saved the heroine from dishonour. During the shooting of this scene Keaton also managed to overturn two cameras, knock out Eddie Cline and demolish a car"[6].

Not only did Keaton not use a stand-in himself, but he stood in for his partners as well. Thus he was also the policeman motor-

---

[6] André Martin, op cit., p. 22.

cycle driver who falls off during the drive, which explains how it is that Keaton remains alone on the handlebars of a speeding machine.[7]

The final result of Keaton's physical courage and temerity did not always leave him unscathed. The motorcycle scene earned him some "beautiful falls" as he described them, and while doing another scene in *Sherlock Junior* he literally "broke his neck".

Keaton did not take such risks merely to show off his physical prowess, to give added spice to his films, or to satisfy contractual clauses. The point is that despite his modesty and his rather frail appearance, Keaton, on the screen, performs wonders as easily as he breathes.[8]

And exceptional as these acrobatic stunts may be, they are no more so than any of the countless other things he is constantly doing in his films. Not only does he jump from bridges, scale mountains, struggle upstream against raging torrents, perform dangerous leaps over roaring cascades and, in short, fly through the air with the greatest of ease, but he also has a go at almost every sport: baseball *(The Cameraman, College)*, American football *(The Three Ages, Seven Chances)*, swimming and rowing *(Sherlock Junior, Our Hospitality, The Navigator, Battling Butler, Seven Chances, The Cameraman, College, Steamboat Bill Junior)*, athletics *(The Cameraman, Seven Chances, Go West, College)*, boxing *(Battling Butler)*, mountain climbing *(Sherlock Junior, Our Hospitality, The Three*

---

[7] "But you know, I was the cop who falls off the motorcycle. I stood in for him because he didn't know how to fall, and I gave my clothing to my prop man". (Interview cited, *Cinéma 60*, p. 70).

[8] Keaton's modesty is such that spectators may be prone to suspect that his acrobatic feats (and those of other early cinema comics, for that matter) are merely examples of trick photography. Of course close examination reveals the contrary to be true, and only increases the value of his performance.

Above: OUR HOSPITALITY. Below: SHERLOCK JR.

THE NAVIGATOR.

Ages), horseback riding *(Paleface* and, despite an unfortunate début, *Go West)*, and, last, chariot racing and dinosaur riding[9] *(The Three Ages)*.

Most constantly striking about his performance is not so much the marvels he performs as the ease with which he performs them, his sheer physical beauty and grace. Placed — more often than not against his better wishes — in situations in which others would either break all their bones or at least emerge exhausted, physical wrecks, Keaton ever expends a smooth and easy energy, with never a breathless effort. He may have to submit to provisional defeat, but he accepts that defeat as he would victory, with the same muscular poise, precision and decisiveness of gesture. And his tense energy assures us that his defeat is indeed only provisional and that, in the end, he will remain unshaken. When necessary, he can turn clumsy tumbles into graceful ballets. Making lyric dives of the worst of them, he can also, thanks to his body's calm, endless energy, turn what would appear to be an atrocious torture into a delightful promenade.[10]

No matter what Keaton does, he never does it in a disjointed fashion. And if his strength, energy and grace are most evident in just those situations wherein, as André Martin acutely observes, "no spectator could claim to do better in similar circumstances,"[11] there is nothing surprising about them. On the contrary, they seem only natural, for Keaton's concentrated energy is constant, and they are thus the natural result of the potential for force, energy and beauty, all concentrated in his slender frame.

[9] A favourite sport among cave men.

[10] In *The Three Ages* a mammoth elephant drags him for several days over stones and thorns. Not only that, but he returns from this "ride" wearing a slight air of triumph beneath his impassive exterior, as if he had reason to thank the elephant for an interesting excursion.

[11] "Le Mécano de la Pantomime", *Cahiers du Cinéma*, no. 86, August 1958, p. 25

The *supremacy* of Keaton's body is inherent in its form and its comportment. Its *structure* as a cinematic object is what emerges from this acrobatic equilibrium.

Taken as a play of line and a moving object in space, Keaton's body is a musical staff from which unrolls a subtle gymnastic melody, a visual music. The achievement of this delicately balanced, constantly harmonious music implies a fund of extraordinary energy, force, precision, rigour and tenacity, all existing in both the conception and the creation.[12] Keaton's slightest gesture is as Olympian and full of energetic intensity as his most explosive outburst.

The force, agility and determination displayed in difficult situations show why Keaton is master of easy ones, just as the concentrated tension and energy manifest in less arduous situations show why he is master of difficult ones. And vice-versa.

Certain themes and *motifs* run through all Keaton's body pantomime, and a brief glance at some of them will enable us to appreciate his rhythm and movement more easily.

RUNNING

Keaton's body is almost never in repose; he gambols and leaps through his films as easily as he breathes — and he seems to have no end of breath! Some of his films, like *Seven Chances* and *Go West*, are veritable marathons. *The General* gives us a splendid example of his incessant activity, here to one single purpose: running along the train from truck to truck, jumping from the guard's van to the tender, jumping from the train to the ground to change the rail-points and clambering back up again — as if he sent himself

---

[12] Cf. André Martin's remarkable analysis of the relation between Keaton's and Chaplin's pantomime. "Le Mécano de la Pantomime", *Cahiers du Cinéma*, no. 86, August 1958.

spinning like a yoyo towards a definite goal and, mission accomplished, jerked the string and rolled back up again.

In his films, Keaton has two ways of running. The first is an almost normal speeding up of his way of walking, a kind of wagging strut that is both supple and full of power and authority[13]; this stride conforms to the terrain; like the little jolting train in *Our Hospitality*, it continues its imperturbable charming way through the country, at the mercy of every pothole and bump. It is a stride which is an end in itself; pleased with itself, it never really tries to get anywhere. It is perfection in itself, the joy of running, the merging and fusing of the body in the space it runs through. It is its own expression, its own fulfillment. It is the way Keaton runs in *Battling Butler* and at the beginning of *Our Hospitality*.

The second way of running might be called Keaton-the-arrow. Here he progresses like the locomotive in *The General*, headlong and swiftly. The stride is straight and certain. It is imperial: the torso rigid, the head high, the eyes straight ahead, concentrating on some point in the distance which only they can see. It is inexorably precise, inflexibly determined in its trajectory. With or without the aid of a high-speed machine, Keaton is a forward-moving force.

At the end of *Our Hospitality* he keeps up pace with the unleashed torrent that carries his love along; in *Go West* he catches up with a stampeding herd of cattle and brings it to order; in *Seven Chances* only the inexhaustibility of his breath, the sureness of his footwork and the energy and persistence of his flight enable him first to escape the furious females who are after his flesh (if I may use the expression) and then the dogged stubborn onrush of enormous

---

[13] When he walks Keaton shows so great a rigidity of the limbs (not of his comportment) and so great a restrained impetuosity, that he seems to arch his legs forward, "something which, nevertheless, the knees do not permit", as André Martin has so justly observed. (Ibid).

boulders in avalanche which pursue him one mad evening. At the end of *Seven Chances*, desperate to save his fortune by arriving at his wedding on time, Keaton performs a dazzling sprint around the obstacles that would block his path, finally bursting through the church door and strewing around him all the garden shrubbery that couldn't resist his speed, drive and determination. In *College* he flies to the aid of his girl in the arms of a monstrous seducer. And in *The Cameraman* he performs an Olympic race and arrives, hardly breathless, at the home of the girl he has just finished speaking to on the telephone, before she has even had time to hang up. Keaton is perhaps never so wonderful as when he is running like this, as when he races like a meteor towards his inexorable goal.

FLYING

Not only can Keaton leap across bridge boards without coming to harm, but he gives proof in the leap of a dazzling elasticity. His legs work like vigorous springs and endow him with an astounding bounce as well as a force and stability in the initial preparation. In *The General* he leaps from the truck attached to his locomotive to the tender, and from the tender to his driver's cabin with a graceful curve that brings him with an almost teleguided precision to his destination. The unequal length of the successive leaps proves that the certainty of his trajectory owes nothing to tricks, and everything to his muscular mastery.

But it is in his aerial ballets that Keaton attains perhaps the highest point in choreographical geometry.

During a fraternity hazing in *College*, Keaton is tossed into the air on a blanket. Suddenly he opens an umbrella and descends slowly and gracefully. Falling from a mountain top in *Paleface*, he once again contrives to make himself a parachute, this time from the blanket he was cloaked in as a disguise.

At another point in *Paleface*, Keaton tumbles, slips and bounces down a long mountain slope. He makes a springboard of the bottom of the slope and bounces from it into a tree, out of the range of his Indian pursuers.[14]

The remarkable motorcycle ballet in *Sherlock Junior* belongs incontestably to the realm of aerobatics. As does, too, Keaton's brilliant flight on a tree at the end of *Steamboat Bill Junior;* Keaton is, to all appearances, a plaything of the elements but in truth he uses them to perform a free and wild ballet and, royal in the wind, ends by taming the tempest.

And how many more such moments exist in these films wherein Keaton, defying gravity, imposes his sovereign liberty on the world![15]

Keaton shows so great a sureness in his trajectory and, it seems, so hidden a purpose, that his changes of direction are brutal and come without any forewarning.[16] And thus it often happens that,

[14] The Indians, like firemen, hold out a blanket for Keaton to jump into and save himself from an unpleasant situation. *Paleface* therefore lays the groundwork for the abovementioned gag in *College*. Actually this gag was already used once before, with firemen, in *The Garage*, one of the first films that Keaton made with Arbuckle. But if the gags are similar in *College* and *Paleface*, it is nevertheless necessary to point out that Keaton uses them differently each time, and changes them accordingly. Far from reflecting creative sterility, this shows how much he polished and repolished his gags in his short films, bringing them to perfection in his long ones.

[15] Let us note here that if Keaton constantly performs wonders in the air, he is generally less at ease in the water; his adjustment to it is usually devious and questionable *(The Navigator)* and more often than not he has great trouble mastering this treacherous element. His vessels usually eject him *(Battling Butler, Sherlock Junior, The Boat* — particularly with its magnificent finale). It is usually only by dint of great determination that he manages to impose his law on the liquid element. And yet, if Keaton is here less brilliant than in the air, water rarely gets the best of him and certainly never vanquishes his indomitable spirit *(College, The Navigator, Our Hospitality, Steamboat Bill Junior)*.

[16] By the same token, Keaton rarely gives any indication that he is about to start out on a race. In *Paleface*, with dangerous Indians infesting the territory, Keaton suddenly bursts into a sprint which stops as suddenly as it began, before we even know what happened. (He had gone to chase a butterfly).

without slowing down one whit, he suddenly swerves, head lowered, and continues in a totally different direction.[17]

Or else he merely stops short, comes to an abrupt halt without warning, and yet does so with such precision, such certainty, that one feels the whole action must have been carefully planned in advance.

In *Paleface*, having eluded his pursuers, Keaton returns to the Indian camp; he stumbles into the clearing and comes face to face with the Indian chief over whose belly he stops short in his famous, characteristic oblique position. A similar incident takes place in *The General* when, at the end of a long run through the night, he comes upon a cabin which is nothing other than the Northern head-quarters, and is literally catapulted and frozen into this oblique position, his face at window level, his hands and chin pressed against the sill, his feet planted in the earth, his whole body so rigid that one almost expects to see it vibrate like the handle of a knife thrown into wood.

In *The General*, Keaton, disguised, finds himself in a queue of Northern soldiers loading a truck; when he comes up to the truck he turns at a right angle and continues on his way, without having given any indication of his intention to do so or permitted anyone to know "just when and how the idea to change direction had taken place".[18] But the geometrical precision of Keaton's manoeuvre, the

---

[17] Cf. J. Schmitz: "He has an absolute control of his muscles which enables him to run, head down, in a given direction, to stop short and take off in the opposite direction without giving any impression that he has retraced his steps, and without moving one facial muscle". *Cahiers du Cinéma*, no. 86, August 1958, "Buster sur le qui-vive: 12".

"He can break his stride, step aside and change direction in mid-stream without any apparent effort, as if these changes of speed were mechanical . . ." André Martin, op. cit. p. 22.

Cf. also: "Every attitude seems seized in flight, caught in action to give way to a movement in an opposite direction". J. P. Coursodon: "Buster Keaton le conquérant solitaire", *Cinéma 58*, no. 30, Sept-Oct. 1958, p. 31.

[18] J. P. Coursodon, op. cit., p. 31.

42

working of his uncanny teleguider, awes us all the more when we realise that he has now stopped at the precise spot which will enable Annabelle to stick her head and arms out of the sack and uncouple the truck from the rest of the train. We are dazed by the clocklike perfection of this movement, what it leads to and the way it leads to it, all presupposing great determination and calculation on Keaton's part, for he evidently knew *beforehand* exactly how much time it would take the loading officer to realise he had changed direction and how much time it would take the officer to summon him back; taking all this into consideration *beforehand*, he fixed his rhythm so as to arrive at the necessary spot and complete the necessary business with a mechanical precision. But he alone knew all this, for we certainly did not[19]; and we are dazzled by this display of precision and mastery of movement at the very moment that they are being accomplished. By multiplying these brusque changes of direction and imperceptible though sudden modifications, one gets a glimpse of those moments of (usually quickly controlled) panic and gestural confusion into which Keaton falls at times and during which he carries out a whole chain of discontinuous movements, all broken before they have hardly been sketched out; as, for instance, the sudden dizzying flight in *The General* which comes to just as sudden a stop, and a return to the original position, or the famous scene in *Our Hospitality* when, half to deceive his opponent, half to give himself courage, Keaton goes through a series of "nonchalant" poses (putting his hands in his pockets, scratching his head, whistling, etc.) all of which form a self-stifling, self-perpetuating chain.

---

[19] Let us call to mind André Martin's statement that: "if Keaton hides his plans and feelings from us, that is not because he is dissimulating them, but because he himself is action, action only". Op. cit. *Cahiers du Cinéma*, no. 86, p. 25.

André Martin writes: "Functioning with a rigorous equilibrium, Keaton's body evolves with a continuous planetary motion"[20]. The examples we have offered only support this definition.

Every change of Keaton's position is a revolution in the astronomical sense of the word inasmuch as it is of a mathematical precision and an absolute rigour. The mineral quality in the sculptural perfection of his face and form confirms this meteorological character. Keaton has the gravity of stone, the gravitation of the planets.

But it would be wrong to liken him to a robot, even were one to liken him to the most highly perfected mechanical robot possible. The precision, rigour, perfection and achievement of his gestures and trajectories are not determined by some greater power exterior to him, but, on the contrary, are the fruits of an auto-dynamism and an unparalleled intensity. He is a pendulum whose oscillations are at one and the same time conception and creation, prediction and event. His bodily equilibrium and precision of movement are above all due to his muscular energy. If Keaton seems to follow an itinerary as implacably as an automatic pilot that is because he is moved by so great a force from within, fed by such power of concentrated energy, that nothing seems capable of stopping him; then, too, his reflective attitude and the constant tenseness of his muscles ensure him a permanent awareness of things and an ability to modify his actions at any given moment. The astronomical precision of his movements comes from an absolute control and mastery of his body which is the sign, not of submission to astrological fatality, but of a supreme freedom which enables him constantly to defy the laws of gravity and equilibrium.

A celestial body, Keaton is the sun emitting its own energy, regulating its own particular movement and imposing itself on the uni-

[20] A. Martin, op. cit. p. 22.

44

verse according to a supple and inflexible trajectory, inexorably alive, intensely alive, attentively alive in an elegant and superb visual self-accomplishment.

*   *   *

The calm insolence of Keaton's movements, his fragile self-confidence, his tense energy in his determined race towards a fixed goal, tend to be sublimated, to be resolved — so as to ensure themselves in concentrated form a whole, definitive perfection — into moments of moving gracefulness.

If *The Cameraman*'s fantastic race seemed, in its perfection, to want to deny movement through instantaneous self-accomplishment and thus to be for once and for all the eternal expression of its self-achievement, with Keaton, inversely, movement tends to freeze into motionlessness — motionlessness which is the expression of motion in resumé, coiled tight like a spring — moments of still and superb balance which seem to want to burst into motion. These motionless poses tend towards dynamism, expressing as they do the balance between Keaton's tense energy and space itself; situated well beyond the normal balance of forces, they are the marvellous sign of Keaton's extraordinary intensity.

As, for example, Keaton's position at the back of the boat in *College*, his back holding the rudder immersed, his body projecting out of the boat, arms and legs taut and gripping the gunwhale, all his being a striving to break the curve of his back, his head thrust forward, extended by the megaphone, stretching towards the bow.

Or Keaton hanging onto the bus from outside in *The Cameraman*, his head level with that of his girl-friend seated inside, his body acrobatically balanced, body and face motionless, impassive and grave, his look lost in distant contemplation.

45

Or Keaton balanced on his locomotive's foot-plate in *The General*, his right leg taut, his left leg folded back as he holds an enormous beam in his folded but not rigid arms, and remains thus, head up, all his energy concentrated, his look deep and grave. The dignity of this pose, in the harmony and balance of his body-line and the beam-line, can only be compared to that of the crucifixion.

Or Keaton scrutinizing the endless sea in *The Navigator*, his body detached and standing out against the horizon as, remarkably balanced, it forms a 45° angle with the rigging.

This bisecting position can also be seen in *Our Hospitality* when Keaton stands in his oblique marbleness atop a cliff, facing the open sea; *The General* also has him presenting the sharp lines of his rigid body in an oblique challenge to the wind as he stands on the roof of his locomotive, shading his eyes with a hand and scrutinizing the distance.

And, lastly, this oblique position is adopted during the typhoon in *Steamboat Bill Junior* when, feet planted firmly in the muddy ground, Keaton presents his brow to the squall, forming a perfectly balanced composition with the bales and crates being swept along by the wind like a shower of heavy confetti, threatening him and responding to him visually. Confronted by this image of determination, will, energy, acrobatic ease, concentration, ultimate body poise, high intensity, attention and openness to the world, all magnificently concentrated and expressed in one sole attitude, we already know that Keaton will soon rise from the earth in superb, composed flight, that he will dominate the tempest and rescue his fiancée, her father and the boat from the raging elements.

If, as F. Scott Fitzgerald writes in *Tender is the Night*, "the cars of a funicular are on the same oblique angle as the hat of a man who does not want to be recognized", Buster Keaton's oblique stance is an expression of tenacity, openness towards great spaces, and intensity, both in tension and attention.

These poses are pauses (the oblique position is without doubt the most perfect and expressive pause imaginable[21]) and, as such, are static sketches of Keaton's dynamic attitude towards the world. These privileged body expressions come across in a sort of vertiginous equilibrium to express, visually, Keaton's dynamic attitude towards reality. They are moments of grace during which he seems to crystallise into poses[22], just as his face sometimes seems to be crystallised. This "perfect geometry"[23], these instants of supreme equilibrium, challenge motion at the very moment when they are motion's most perfect expression.

Having examined Keaton's *visual* side which is a characteristic of his personality, it remains for us to examine his *dynamic* side which s a characteristic of his behaviour, as a comic character, in the world. This behaviour expresses itself in the gag.

---

[1] This becomes most apparent if one considers the photo taken during the shooting of *The Buster Keaton Story*, reproduced on p. 130 in no. 30 (Sept.-Oct.) of *Cinéma 58*.

Buster Keaton and Donald O'Connor, who plays him in the film, stand side by side in this famous position. O'Connor, who knows how to twist his body into a great number of remarkable positions (cf. his solo in Donen's *Singin' in the Rain*), suffers badly by the comparison.

Keaton's body, thrust infinitely further forward than O'Connor's, also offers a unity which O'Connor's lacks altogether. The arch of his legs is much greater and steadier (he really does seem rooted in the earth by the solid stalk of his legs); his torso is straighter and much more on an axis with his body; his folded arms form, with the general curve of his pose, an harmonious balance which seems to solder them to the trunk, whereas O'Connor's arms seem anxious to abandon this position as soon as possible. And, lastly, O'Connor's head is bowed whereas Keaton's head is high, and Keaton's face (although aged and wrinkled) retains its marble-like grandeur and its impenetrable unity, beside which the light grimace that deforms O'Connor's features seems like a monstrous caricature.

Let us remark in passing that certain *rapports* between Keaton and O'Connor do not begin with *The Buster Keaton Story*. Keaton himself sang in the rain as long ago as 1929, in *The Hollywood Revue*.

[22] This is no reason to consider him a *Poseur*.

[23] The inverted commas return this expression to its legitimate owner, André Martin, although he used it in a more general sense.

By analysing his behaviour we shall be better equipped to understand that which the crystalline beauty of his visual attitudes reduced and concentrated; the visual examination has already revealed one of Keaton's inalienable qualities: a dignity, a supremacy and a concealed mastery which nothing can take away. If we keep this in mind, we shall not be too surprised by certain curious turns that Keaton may take in his encounters with the world.

But first we must look at Keaton from yet another angle, after which we shall watch his behaviour in the world with even greater understanding.

3. A Great Director

(Assuming a "world action")

> "Directing is not how things are extra-ordinary
> but how they are extraordinary."
> Berthe Olbrèche

A PART from the sheer beauty of his body's movement in space, Keaton, with his consummate skill at synthesis and linear composition, manages to handle objects so that they seem like normal extensions of his body. Vehicles are evidently the privileged objects in this sense: old and curious bicycles *(Our Hospitality, The General)*, hand-carts *(The General)*, motorcycles *(Sherlock Junior)*, beds and trees *(Steamboat Bill Junior);* and then, of course, there are the great machines, whole mechanised worlds with unlimited mechanical possibilities: the liner in *The Navigator*, the little train in *Our Hospitality*, and the greatest train of all, his beloved *General* itself.

Keaton and his different means of locomotion become one body, not only in terms of action, but also by the graceful form which that action takes. Here tense energy (clumsiness and catastrophe notwithstanding) confers on the single object that is the vehicle + Keaton a matchless beauty and nobility.

The body alone is not the sole source of this perfect delineation, this "perfect geometry". The linear balance covers the whole canvas. The perfect integration of Keaton's body in the space around him is not the result of one particular autonomous quality, but rather of the positioning of each individual pictorial element, and particularly the positioning of that principal element around which the picture is organised: Keaton's body.

When Keaton (standing oblique on the roof of his machine) and his locomotive drive through nature, the beauty and expressiveness of this shot is not uniquely due to Keaton and his extension, the machine, but to the countryside being travelled through as well.

If we look once again at his oblique position in *Steamboat Bill Junior*, we immediately understand what his beauty and finely etched spatial equilibrium represent. Indeed, the vertiginous balance in which this shot seems to crystallise all Keaton's virtualities and make them sublime, comes not only from his oblique position, but also from the visual counterpoint to his position as represented by the shower of bales and crates themselves feeling the pull of gravity and, as it were, suspended in the air for the space of a second.

The perfection and beauty of Keaton's form in space comes not merely from the serene equilibrium inherent in his body, but above all from its positioning in cinematic space, a perfect, harmonious positioning, marvellously suggesting and expressing his body's potential for power and balance. This positioning, which is nothing other than the directing of the film, reveals Keaton-personality and Keaton-attitude perfectly and translates them into physical and visual terms. One says "translates", but the word is badly chosen, for these qualities exist nowhere else and in no other way. The film itself has created them. The natural harmony of Keaton's body, added to the harmony of the overall positioning, creates those very virtues, victorious balance and integration, which are characteristic of the "perfect geometry" of Keaton's visual existence in space.

All the examples given during the examination of the visual and physical aspects[1] of Keaton in motion plainly showed, though we made no attempt to stress it, how his body's structure tends to form spatial lines, the horizons, natural inclines, objects and moving bodies that people the canvas,[2] organising all into a sort of geometrical ballet, into great engineering games in which choreographical perfection is wedded to mechanical precision.

Keaton's profoundly visual kind of comedy depends on his skill in directing which permits him to use space itself as an element in his gags. And thus by using different shots of a railway track describing a hairpin bend on a steep slope together with shots of a locomotive prankishly advancing and retreating, Keaton can gallop through woods, tumble down the slope and scale rocks (*The General*). Ultimately this turns into a sort of abstract locomotive ballet. Using an ingenious system of deceptively crossing railway tracks (one of the two, no longer in use, is suspended in the air), Keaton then superposes two trains going at top speed, one forward, the other (his, the General) backward, and after having led us to believe the two will inevitably crash, he isolates one train perched on its track in a ridiculous, grotesque position, as the other, roaring forward, disappears.

Keaton makes the Northerners who pursue him look ridiculous, and uses scenic elements to jeer at them: by his retreat which suddenly reveals how to avoid a crash as well as the grotesque position in which the Northerners now find themselves, he makes them look ridiculous; by placing his train directly beneath their shelf, out of their reach, he seems to be there deliberately to jeer at them.

The mad humour of this scene rests on a genuine visual pun, the result of mathematically precise direction.

[1] Moreover opening on to a moral attitude.

[2] Sometimes, even, when he is not present.

In the same token, Keaton knows how to confer a matchless grace on a locomotive crashing through a flaming bridge and taking the bridge with it as it plunges, with loose abandon, to the bottom of the river; as it goes under the locomotive snorts one last puff of steam, a final reproach to the Northern general who claimed the bridge was crossable.

The arrival of the Northern troops and the battle in *The General* are such triumphs of direction that this scene attains an epic dimension. The same holds true for the Southern army's retreat and the Northern army's parade, through which Keaton wanders oblivious (or, rather, of which he becomes aware only later).

These scenes from *The General* are famous enough as they are. There's little need to dwell on them.[3]

There is, in *Paleface*, apart from the scenes of horseback riding in the woods and the marvellous shot of Keaton, his costume exchanged for an oil bandit's, impeccable in his handsome dinner jacket, disappearing into the bottom of a quarry with an elegance paradoxically suited to the quarry's majesty, one particular gag which comes of Keaton's use of spatial line. We have already mentioned it but let us look at it in greater detail.

Keaton is descending a precipitous slope, pursued by Indians; he uses the bottom of the slope, which becomes horizontal and slightly inclined, as a springboard which catapults him into a tree. The use of the diagonal (the slope), the horizontal (the springboard) and the vertical (the tree) already reveal in Keaton a sense of line which is

[3] Cf. C. Miller: "The same spatial wideness, the same ample, serene, indeed epic respiration (the battle on Rock River is a veritable bit of epic cinema) unite the two films". *(Télé-Ciné* no. 107, Oct.-Nov., 1962. Entry on *le Mécano de la Générale)* and André Martin: "The scenic beauty, the width and depth of the locations directly complement the dynamism of the action. One of the most extraordinary "adventure film" images in all cinema is certainly the one in *The General* wherein the Northern locomotive, crossing a flaming bridge, demolishes it and plunges into a river full of panic-stricken soldiers". *(Cahiers du Cinéma,* op cit.).

THE GENERAL.

53

LE MÉCANO DE LA GÉNÉRALE
Le Chef-d'œuvre comique de BUSTER KEATON

THE GENERAL.

irresistibly comic and at the same time extremely beautiful. But this is not all. Next come the Indians who surround the tree and hold out a blanket for him to jump into. He jumps and, as if the blanket were a drum skin stretched taut, bounces from it on to the overhang which forms the base of the slope. And this time, scaling the same slope he descended only moments ago, he once again escapes from the Indians. The same movements have been repeated, but this time backwards.[4]

In *The Cameraman* we see Keaton impatiently awaiting a telephone call from the girl he loves. On the screen we are given a section of his house and an outline of the staircase. Each time the 'phone rings[5] Keaton sets out on a frantic run to answer it. The first time, he ends up in the cellar. The second time, he runs too high and bursts out on the roof; navigating the curve of the landing, he climbs the slope of a penthouse which just happened to be there and just happened to have the same incline and outline as the staircase.

All remember the famous scene from *The Navigator*, described by André Martin[6], in which Keaton and the girl run after each other without ever managing to meet. The chase develops "according to subtly controlled progressions"[7] horizontally: the two running on different decks; and vertically: climbing up or down from the two decks to a third, middle deck — and seems to resolve itself diagonally, on the stairways that lead from one deck to another. Added to these variations on different levels are variations on different depths as the two race forwards and backwards (with the confluent

[4] And a bit to the right: the point of impact on the blanket which forms the summit of the angle constructed by the lines Keaton describes, is displaced towards the right in respect to the base of the slope.

[5] Never, incidentally, for him.

[6] "Le Mécano de la Pantomime", *Cahiers du Cinéma*, no. 86, August 1958, p. 28.

[7] Ibid.

theme of all the cabin doors in the background opening and closing in unison to the roll of the boat, like a full orchestra answering solo instruments (Keaton and the girl) in a concerto). Variations on time, the result of progressive acceleration, are added to this use of line to make of this scene a ballet of extraordinary visual music.

But we have so far considered these spatial lines as more or less abstract diagrams; and Keaton is never so great as when he manages to organise (to seize simply) the countryside into his overall design, giving, in a flashing surge of beauty, his personal vibration to the secret modulation of its lines, to its concrete harmony — as when he gallops indefatigably through the antediluvian country of *Seven Chances*, or that shot from *Battling Butler* in which, in a kind of immense and muddy lunar circus, one sees Keaton's small but steady silhouette reduced to two legs at the ends of which two enormous muddy masses — his feet — run towards a horizon far in the distance out of sight.

These images give birth to both laughter and overwhelming beauty, each of which nourishes the other. These images are the affirmation of this body which imposes itself on the world and fits so perfectly into space. Keaton runs to embrace this world which belongs to him and to which he belongs; it is because his is a match for the unleashed elements in *Steamboat Bill Junior*, for example, that he succeeds in taming them.

"Keaton is probably the only comic who, apart from the classic race-chase, really knows how to use space, to give wing to the gag, to burst the bonds of the 'inside gag' by blowing a great wind into it, filling it with countryside and endless vistas, finally organising the universe into an immense gag in itself"[8].

[8] As P. Demun very aptly remarked, "Espace Vital", in *Contre-Champ*, no. 3, May 1962, review of *Steamboat Bill Junior* and *Battling Butler*.

The serene, fantastic and matchless beauty which emanates from the way he organises the universe are the marks of his poetic genius.

But none of these marvellous images, these moments of beauty which spring at us in forests, city streets and rocky amphitheatres are the results of any systematic search for "beautiful shots". Keaton is not of those who confuse directing with pretty images[9].

There is no fancy-work, nothing designed "to impress" in his films. He is not one of those who, contemptuous of the comic cinema, feels obliged to give it a bit of dignity, to make of it an "art film" by using remarkable photographic effects and adding brilliant supporting players. Buster Keaton's cinema is elegant; but it is never precious. The beauty of his films is, like all real beauty, involuntary but necessary; for the perfect geometry and the visual supremacy inherent in all of Keaton's images are functional. They are the inevitable product of Keaton's intensity (which they resolve) and the world around him. And Keaton's directing is the directing of his behaviour in the world; it is the literal *positioning* of his

---

[9] We think it unnecessary to remind readers that Buster Keaton was the real director of his films. But, if need be, their overall coherence, their stylistic coherence, would suffice to prove it. This stylistic coherence is not merely recognisable by Keaton's presence (for Keaton is himself a style, a way of being in the world) but by the way in which this presence manifests itself cinematically. All of his films, whether he made them with Eddie Cline, Charles F. Reisner, Donald Crisp, Edward Sedgwick, Clyde Bruckman or W. Horne as official of associate directors, resemble the man around whom they centre, namely Keaton himself. And there is little difference to be found between the films he made in collaboration and the films he made on his own. A director who is also an actor obviously requires someone to stand behind the camera and see that all works according to plan, but it is nevertheless true that both the impetus and the style were Keaton's. "I was not always the director, or the sole director, of my films. But I worked actively on elaborating the scenarios and selecting the gags and that's why all my films have, I believe, a family resemblance. When I worked with a co-director he stayed beside the camera and followed the shooting of the scene, all the details of which we had first worked out carefully together, and told me later if everything had gone as planned or if, somewhere in the background, without my knowledge, something had gone badly." ("A Quatre Temps", in *Cahiers du Cinéma*, no. 130, April 1962, p. 30).

Then, too, let's not forget that Keaton edited his films himself and wrote his own scenarios. In other words, he invented his own gags. "*When did you first begin to edit your films yourself?*" 'When I began to shoot my films myself. Arbuckle taught me how to edit. He edited his own films." ("Interview with Buster Keaton" by Christopher Bishop, *Cinéma 60*, no. 49, August-September 1960, p. 70).

action. With nothing extraneous added, Keaton's *positioning* enables him to "accomplish" his action and give it its form.

Though Keaton's work abounds in touches of genius which can often be related to that category known as "brilliant directorial finds", he never introduces anything extraneous for its own sake; everything relates to, and helps to further, the story-action. When, in *The General*, the pursuing Northern army's locomotive comes up behind Keaton's guard's van and the enemy soldiers can be seen leaning forward on the foot-plate to couple their train to his, the camera smoothly continues panning the length of the guard's van in question and, arriving at the other end, shows us Keaton in the process of uncoupling it himself from his own locomotive. The ultimate object of this pan shot is not so much to surprise us into laughter at this gag[10] as to prepare us for the eventual discomfiture of the poor souls who have no idea what they're in for when they try matching themselves against Keaton, and come up against situations for which they've been extremely ill-prepared. We are also given an opportunity to appreciate the subtlety of Keaton's revenge; for whereas the Northerners, on the first lap of this round-trip voyage, only complicated things for him by leaving an un-hitched truck on the track, he now more or less uses their own technique against them, but much more efficaciously and much more perfectly, all of which proves that he is not merely capable of turning the tide in his favour, but can do so with incomparable brio.

When, in *Steamboat Bill Junior*, by a simultaneous rotation in opposite directions of two barber chairs by two young barbers,

[10] Which would, incidentally, be perfectly legitimate and laudable. In any event, the gag would be inconceivable without a certain element of surprise, and there's no doubt that the pan shot is part of the gag. Nevertheless, the quality of surprise is slightly impure here, revealing as it does (and brutally so) the results of an action the premises of which had been hidden from us. But with Keaton the result of an action is almost always confused with the action itself, for he never plays on suspense.

Keaton finds himself face to face with the girl with whom he falls immediately in love, what we have is not merely a simple directing trick, but rather a veritable *presentation through positioning*, the visual equivalent of love at first sight.[11]

The way Keaton perceives a scene through "a frame of a folded arm"[12], and the way the trainer's body hides Keaton until the former steps aside to reveal him *(Battling Butler)* are absolutely functional and necessary visions, being the physical and spatial expression of a moment in Keaton's life, the translation in physical terms of a moral relationship[13].

In *Seven Chances*, after numerous rejections, Keaton stands beneath his girl's balcony and proposes marriage one last time, writing the question on a piece of paper and throwing it up to her. Motionless, the camera remains on Keaton; soon after, his little billet-doux descends on him in shreds. This sublime visual moment does not play on coquetry and suspense; quite simply, the camera must stay on him; it has nowhere else to go. We know that he has no illusions; and what matters now is he himself, his reaction, his act itself and not the act of the girl rejecting him. And this becomes

[11] This is assuredly one of the most beautiful examples of love at first sight in the cinema.
   Keaton's concentration on what he is doing, his attention to what he is doing (and not his distraction of blindness) is often such that he does not concentrate on, or pay attention to, anything else. Hazard must then reveal treasures to him. But let a turning chair suddenly put him in the presence of beauty, and his look will show us plainly the intense wonder he can find in reality.

[12] Cf. "While Keaton trains for the ring in *Battling Butler*, he espies, in the triangle formed by the referee's folded arm and hand on hip, his girl friend bantering with his rival. The framing suggests impotent jealousy. Not only is Keaton forced to remain an onlooker at a scene which directly involves him and involves him sentimentally, but the spatial arrangement also indicates so well the particular conditioning of his conflict, the referee's arm between him and his girl being the 'trial of power' imposed on him if he is to 'merit' her." ("Le plus bel animal du monde", Michel Mardore, *Cahiers du Cinéma*, no. 130, April 1962, p. 34).

[13] Here, too, the word "translation" is hardly apt, for this moral relationship does not exist independent of the physical one (opposing the imposing trainer's body to Keaton's frail form completely hidden by it); on the contrary, it is the physical relationship alone that exists. The "translation" is thus most effective, but in the other sense.

even more evident when Keaton — who also reveals here his sensitivity to all things — raises his collar as the shreds of paper begin to fall, until they cover his shoulders like snow.

But there is no need to look for exceptional moments to praise Keaton's consummate directorial artistry; every example we have given of Keaton's "perfect geometry", of his sense of linear organisation and of the way his body fits so perfectly in space is ample proof that Keaton's direction is above all the *positioning in a setting* of a body *in action*, and is evidence of the geometrical precision and the expressive richness of this positioning.

It is Keaton's mastery of space which permits him his "brilliant directorial finds", of which André Martin has said, "Although they use standard cinema techniques unimpeachably, they avail themselves of a liberty of sequence much closer to that of animated films which, with their uniquely graphic technique, have no figurative difficulty." *(Cahiers du Cinéma*, no. 86, August 1958, op cit. p. 25).

Indeed, gags equivalent to saving the heroine from the cascade *(Our Hospitality)*, the motorcycle scene in *Sherlock Junior* and the journey across a picket fence, a fat lady and her street stall in the same film, the use of stairs in *The Cameraman*, the chase in *The Navigator* and the transformation of Keaton into an undamaged Saint Sebastian in *Paleface* — gags equivalent to these scenes are only to be found in animated films.

Take, for example, that gag (described by André Martin) in *Haunted House* which has Keaton opening the double-door of the bank where he works, first by unscrewing the lock with the middle link of his key chain after which, inserting the key, he ends up opening the wing of the door that had no lock on it.

Cf. Keaton himself: "I never shied away from the most crazy, impossible gag, the kind that was later used by cartoon makers."

("A quatre temps", *Cahiers du Cinéma*, no. 130, April 1962, p. 30).

* * *

André Martin reports a perhaps apocryphal statement attributed to Chaplin: "I'm an extraordinary being; I need no extraordinary angles"[14]. But André Martin then seems to set Keaton against this statement on the pretext that Keaton has a sense of nature that Chaplin lacks. But it seems to us that Chaplin's reasons for almost never appearing in nature and almost never confronting natural elements[15] are more general than that and the reasons for it are what fundamentally differentiates his kind of comedy from Keaton's. The difference between Chaplin and Keaton is more profound than Martin would allow. Chaplin seldom comes to grips with nature because his comedy is the comedy of a socially-determined being whose acts[16] find fulfilment in a social milieu. Keaton is a more elemental comic, which is to say that his acts find their fulfilment in a more natural (in the literal sense of the word) environment; his relations with the world itself are more direct; if he is a "man of the world", that is because his conflict is usually the conflict of man versus object, not man versus man, and his object is often, in this sense, the whole world itself. Keaton thus needs nature.[17]

[14] Op cit., *Cahiers du Cinéma*, no. 86, August 1958, p. 27.

[15] Although in *The Gold Rush*, for example, the mountain, the emptiness and the snow play very important roles. And one cannot deny Chaplin a certain sense of space in that shot in *The Gold Rush* showing a long line of prospectors forming a rut in the snowy mountainside.

[16] These "acts" are often overstated, harming Chaplin's efficacity and drowning it in sentimentality.

[17] This passage, of course, is not intended to be an exhaustive statement on Keaton's kind of comedy. It is both inexact and schematic, but we shall study it more fully later. We merely wanted to point out one aspect of Keaton's comic style which is profoundly different to Chaplin's. In the same token, our "analysis" of Chaplin's comedy is ultra-schematic.

That Keaton, living in a mechanised society, was often led to give his comedy a "cosmic" aspect, concerned as he was from the beginning with the relation of being and object and thus considering the entire world as a sort of object confronting man, is a perhaps preponderant fact; but that's another story.

André Martin's statement can certainly apply to Keaton as well to Chaplin. For indeed Keaton's directing is nothing more than a positioning, with no flourishes, with no "extraordinary angles", of the extraordinary being he incarnates. Keaton, like Chaplin, "considers himself the centre of the action."[18] It is their action that is different, and that takes different forms, and there's the precise difference between them.

Chaplin is mainly *demonstration*. He is above all the *subversive manifestation* of himself. His body is principally the sign of his exuberant presence, with all that that implies. His principal task is therefore to present this sign, to show that it exists. For which reason the camera is almost always focused directly on Chaplin and only occasionally moves back to "take in a wider arabesque."

Keaton is essentially *action* — action upon which his behaviour, his fitting into space and his adjustment to it, depends; the result of this action is seen in relation to its setting. Keaton exists above all in his acts, acts which, like for Chaplin, reveal his character, of course, but which implicate at one and the same time both him and the setting in which his acts take place. And that is why almost all his scenes are shot with the camera taking in a wider area.

Chaplin manages to maintain himself as an explosive manifestation, and remains what he is. He cuts through space like a cataclysm and pays it no heed: Keaton, on the other hand, is a meteor seeking to place itself in orbit. Chaplin's maladjustment is manifest in his face, and not in the relation of his body to its setting; Keaton as a whole is expressed in his body's fitting into the space around it.

The confines of the screen do not stifle Keaton, as they seem to stifle Chaplin, fettering his exuberance. On the contrary, the screen seems to be Keaton's natural habitat. In this sense, given Keaton's

[18] André Martin, op. cit., p. 27.

always harmonious, functional fusing with his settings, he is much less fundamentally a "loner", an "alien" (as some would have us believe) than Chaplin who, cinematically, remains much more of an isolated, alien object.

The appearance of loneliness is, however, in some way inherent in the comic. Laurel and Hardy may well be a duo, the Marx Brothers a trio, they are all nevertheless alone of their type. This apparent loneliness, which some have latched on to in order to pose the thesis of the moral loneliness, of certain comics (maintaining that, like Molière of old, every great comic is "eternally solitary", "desperately lucid", finding his sole consolation in the comic spectacle that is the farce of life, and so on and so forth) [theses much coveted and adored by our intellectual elite] — this apparent loneliness of the comic character is precisely that quality in him which makes him unique; but it goes no farther than that and certainly gives no real indication of the comic's attitude towards the world. Technically speaking, Harold Lloyd with his beatific optimism is just as lonely as Chaplin, Keaton and Langdon, and yet our cherished despair ideologists have never singled him out for this — which would be to let the cat out of the bag. The loneliness of comic characters has no precise ethical value in itself.

Indeed one might say that every comic film is a striving towards non-loneliness: the narration of the journey from alienation to adjustment. What matters first is to show that the comic character's attitude is "possible". And for that, the comic film is not asked to give us the spectacle of happiness already attained and running smoothly. Being a sort of test case, the comic character begins his itinerary over again in every film, for every film is the proof of his existence in a strange and different form, and his possibility for adjustment.

Chaplin's strangeness is, in fact, a manifestation of himself in respect of the social strata which reject him; Keaton, whose conflict, we repeat, is both more general and more particular imposes his strangeness on, and fits it into, the world.

It would be interesting to show how, in the last analysis, Keaton's ability to "fit in" and Chaplin's inability to do so (as each incarnates definitively, in different ways, the same conflicts and the same demands) tend to go in the same direction (but such is not the subject of this book).

Like Chaplin, Keaton needs no "extraordinary angles"; what counts with him is the simplicity of his positioning. Chaplin's statement might also apply to Keaton in another way, presupposing (and affirming) as it does the proposition that the comic is under no obligation to conform to aesthetic forms imposed on him from without and which owe nothing to his own inner effulgence; in this case one is speaking of "extraordinary angles" but one might just as well be talking of dramatic construction. And this raises the question of the importance of the scenario in Keaton's films, and in all comic films in general.

A NOTE ON SCENARIOS IN COMIC FILMS, AND IN THE FILMS OF BUSTER KEATON

It is nothing less than remarkable how the cult of criticism with its rules on construction, etc., handed down from the theatre and the art of rhetoric, has harmed the cinema in its natural development.

Burlesque has always been treated with contempt by critics and "the right sort of people" as being "vulgar" and "inhumane". This was the case during the silent era just as it is the case today. More unfortunate, however, is that the tastes of today's cinema-goers have been so twisted by the basely demagogic "psychological" cinema and by literature-writing critics, that they have come to despise burlesque on the pretext that it lacks "subtlety" whereas this lack of subtlety was precisely what so delighted the cinema-goers of the twenties (and a lot of good it did them). Today, for economic, sociological and many other reasons which it is not our business to analyse here, burlesque has disappeared, and none but cinephiles are left to love and miss the golden age of American burlesque.

Comedy in the cinema relies essentially on one character who brings with him a whole new world of perception, gestures, reactions, etc. and who, coming into contact with the world, himself sets off the fireworks that follow. This being the case, it is utter nonsense to try to construct a scenario according to rules. There is no dramatic idea here to be developed, complicated and resolved! For a comic character, being the incarnation of a fundamental attitude towards reality, does not *develop*. And therefore his very being refuses *dramatic construction* and *scenarios*. By saying he does not develop we do not mean that his behaviour is not dynamic. On the contrary, he is always in action. But his *rapport* with the world, dynamic as it may be, once established is established forever; he has no psychological development, his personality does not change in his dealings with beings and things, he does not readjust himself, for the very good reason that, unlike the dramatic character, he is not in a state of crisis, or, rather, he is in a perpetual state of crisis; he is never quite "with it."

The comic film has no reason to work within the limits of a dramatic line, to wear the yoke of a pre-established, rigid dramatic action.

Let us note in passing that if, as it has been said, "the Marx Brothers never found themselves the right director," the reason for that is, more often than not, because they were condemned to conform to scenarios. *A Night at the Opera*, for instance, is a badly constructed burlesque film precisely because it tries too hard to be a "well constructed" one, and elements totally alien to the Marx Brothers are constantly coming in to try pulling the thing into shape.

The collective comic personality who stars in Mack Sennett's films was content to go out into the street and let what happened happen in its own rhythm. "But that was precisely its weakness!" one will say, "Look how Mack Sennett never could make a full-length film."

Such a remark is not valid; it is precisely because they had no "story" that Mack Sennett's films can be run together. What condemned Sennett to the short was the exhausting pace of his films which no viewer could bear for any length of time.[19] Besides, programmes of Mack Sennett films, made up of several short ones, were the equivalent of long films with intervals, and in this they hardly differed from the serials which were our grandfathers' passion. Each of these short films was, in fact, one episode of a long story that never ended.

A montage film like *The Golden Age of Comedy*, for instance, which is nothing but one big juxtaposition, confirms our view. It is, paradoxically, this film's lack of unity (no attempt was made to give it a unity of tone) which makes us aware of a great coherence. The harmony of the whole was broken by the mixing of many kinds of period films together; but if one isolates the Mack Sennett films (those with Chester Conklin, Hank Mann, Al St. John, etc., and those with Ben Turpin or Will Rogers) one is aware of an extraordinary unity going through them, a unity of style, the style of American burlesque at its roots. An done almost feels, as one leaves

---

[19] Laughing from beginning to end, one might conceivably choke to death if the film lasted longer.

the cinema, that one has seen one single film.

Buster Keaton is no exception to this rule; he is, rather, one of its most perfect illustrations. If the full length film taught him how to handle the spectator and draw the laughter out more slowly, if, therefore, he does construct his films[20], he is fully aware that he alone is the engine that drives this construction along.

All of which is not to say that he began a film with no story outline, that his films were nothing but improvisations worked out on the spur of the moment; rather, he never bothered to apply subtle rules of cause and effect, to let little details get in the way, to do all that is proper and right in dramatic scenarios. As André Martin has accurately said: "Keaton never looked for subtle visual equivalents but had one solid thread going through every action: *He does this and I do that. And then this happens and then*... His scenarios resemble appointment books of busy executives..."[21]

It would be absurd to infer from the above that Keaton used no scenario in the sense of a story progressing through a succession of

---

[20] "The first effect should happen at a precise moment; the audience should then be given the chance to get hold of itself, after which the effect should be carried as far as possible, or the scene should progress, depending on the case. There is a kind of mathematical precision to this rhythm, for it is absolutely imperative that the audience feel the full force of the comic incident and await the next funny moment without the slightest feeling of lassitude. The director must be a specialist in the science of rhythm.
"A comic film is put together, you might say, as carefully as the wheels of a watch. The simplest action, performed too quickly or too slowly, can lead to disaster." ("Buster Keaton, Le Metier de faire rire" in the *Anthologie du Cinéma* by M. Lapierre, Paris, 28 June 1946, p. 355).

Let us not forget the extraordinary liberty granted the first American comics in the shooting of their films; they shot reel after reel, a little of everything, and it was only in the editing that they selected what pleased them to construct their films. "Unlike those others (five act dramas) we used no definite manuscript of any kind; we thought up a thin plot which sufficed to enable us to start building scenery; then we set ourselves to thinking of 'gags' (comic ideas and actions) to fit the situations and the settings. When we felt that we had 'shot' enough for five or six films, we stopped and assembled what we had; by successive cutting we arrived at the desired film, containing all that was best of the lot." (Keaton shot every scene only once and always took the first. We mention this so no-one will think that "enough for five or six films" were rushes). ("Le Metier de faire rire".)

[21] Op. cit., p. 26.

planned incidents.[22] Of course he knew what was going to happen in his films. But the development of the story internally, dynamically, was dependent on, and engendered by, the acts, through gags, of the central character and his own particular way of adjusting to the world. The comic hero must never give the impression that he is yielding to the will of a scenario; rather, he must develop freely according to his own rhythm, his own form, both of which he defines, both of which define him.

Actually, the presence of a scenario should not be felt in "dramatic" films either, for the actions of characters should never appear to be those of puppets on invisible strings.

But comparisons cannot really be made between the two kinds of films, for dramatic films call for much more complex human, psychological and social relations between characters than do comic films; dramatic characters lack the simplicity and, too, the infinite subtlety of comic characters; and whereas the comic film centres around one particular character, the dramatic film almost always brings together several characters of more or less equal importance who, unlike comic characters whose inner beings create situations, are formed by and responsive to external situations. Dramatic characters are victims of dramatic necessity and therefore much less free in their actions than comic characters.

It goes without saying that I am not speaking here of those "psychological French films" and others of their ilk which are nothing but the laborious putting into application of systems of tried and worn banalities.

Bad burlesque films are precisely those in which what happens

---

[22] The comic cinema does not so much destroy the idea of the scenario as a plan of action, as it does of a *dramatic evolution*. When we say that there can be no scenario for a comic film, we are talking of "*the art*" *of the scenario*, i.e. the idea of developing, complicating and resolving an intrigue according to subtly controlled progressions.

does not seem to emanate from the characters, but in which the characters seem to conform to the fluctuations of a scenario. Example: most French "comic" films, or *Hellzapoppin*.

A film like *The Three Ages*, for example, which parodies *Intolerance*, is very well constructed, but lacks the rigour of the latter. For in all three of the ages, what happens depends on what Keaton does, and on the genetic impetus of the action he represents.

The liveliness of every one of Keaton's films is due to what he does and how he reacts to things. There is no foreign interference. Scenes might follow one another in any order whatsoever; Keaton is the constant, the strong thread tying them together, and that thread is never broken.

Most striking about Keaton is precisely the fact that many of his films *are* so well constructed. There is a kind of symmetry in the structure, usually a result of *turnabouts (Convict 13, Electric House, Playhouse, My Wife's Relations, Sherlock Junior, The General, College, The Cameraman*, etc. to mention only a few)[23].

The *turnabout* (which we shall have the opportunity to study in more detail later) is the principal *form* of the relation uniting Keaton to the situations in which he finds himself. Keaton's scenario symmetry is therefore not imposed arbitrarily from without; it is, on the contrary, the natural expression and development of his activity as expressed in the gag. And if this symmetry seems to reflect his taste for geometry, well, a love for geometry is one of Keaton's basic characteristics[24] and it is geometrically that he confronts and controls the world.

[23] As we can see, it is above all in the short films that this structural symmetry lasts from beginning to end. This is because the short films (precisely because they are short) are often based uniquely on the development of one single gag, the film itself, which is shot through with secondary gags.

[24] Both in and out of his films.

André Martin writes: "In all the annals of the comic cinema, the rescue of the heroine in *The General*, inspired, incidentally, by an authentic Civil War exploit, represents, I believe, the most complex and brilliantly handled enterprise ever attempted by a comic hero" . . . "The film unwinds with the energy of a perpetual motion machine around the single axis of a railway line. On the return trip all that happened during the first part happens again, but differently, turning the film over like a coin, as amazing as the far side of the moon; and the abundance of 'finds', of attitudes, and of remarkable images is never diminished"[25]. The symmetry of the construction not only allows Keaton to display an unflagging inventiveness,[26] but is also based uniquely on his actions. The logic of his behaviour and his perseverance in what he is doing are responsible for the film's structural equilibrium. And we are once again witness to the functional use that Keaton the creator puts to what in others might appear to be artifice.

College is probably the only film in which this symmetry is a bit overstressed. The film itself is a *tour de force* which concludes at the end a gag begun at the beginning,[27] as Keaton succeeds in accomplishing all that he originally failed at. And thus two series of gags form one sole gag, stretched out in the middle and enclosing the middle between the premises and the conclusion. The turnabout — original failure becoming final victory — which serves as the film's spring, is perfectly justified, since everything Keaton does in the film comes as the result of his determination to succeed in what he failed at. The film's symmetrical construction is therefore admirable; it is not imposed on Keaton from without, but, on the contrary,

[25] Op. cit., pp. 25 and 28.

[26] As we saw with the train gag.

[27] Or, more exactly, a series of gags.

This and previous page: THE GENERAL.

emanates directly from him.

At the beginning of *College*, unfortunately, Keaton the director decided to spice things and thereby introduced an artificial symmetry.[28] And every time that Keaton the actor appears to compete in an athletic event, Keaton the director feels it necessary to show us *systematically* the normal way to throw a javelin, run a race, pole-vault, etc.[29] This symmetry, showing the exercise as it should be done and then showing it as catastrophically performed by Keaton, inasmuch as it is not the natural outgrowth of Keaton's inner behaviour, seems contrived; this would be relatively unimportant if it did not serve to deprive the gags that follow of their comical efficacity. And so, in every pause between the model performance of the feat and Keaton's taking the stage, one seems to feel the director whisper, as P. Demun remarked, "Watch out! You're now going to see something you don't expect." By taking away the element of surprise, the gag falls flat. And falls all the flatter because as a rule Keaton's impenetrability, which always leaves the spectator wondering what he'll do next, is usually one of the surest laugh factors.

But this slight disappointment at the beginning is amply compensated for by our laughter at the end, when the indomitable Keaton throws weights, leaps hedges and pole-vaults superbly, gloriously triumphing over everything that stymied him earlier on. This time the symmetry is perfect in the comic situation.

The scenario is therefore for Keaton a kind of positioning of

[28] In his review of the film in *Contre-Champ* no. 3, May 1962, P. Demun attributes this "fault" as he calls it to J. W. Horne; but since the penchant for geometry is Keaton's own, it seems rather his fault than that of the nominal director.

[29] "As if Keaton were not from the outset beyond the pale of the normal; it is normal for Keaton to be abnormal; we must show his abnormality normally", as P. Demun has so well said (*Contre-Champ*, no. 3, May 1963, op. cit. "Faute d'arbitrage".)

himself. Instead of imposing on himself the iron collar of formal dramatic construction, he lets the action grow freely out of himself.

Both in his scenarios and his direction Keaton strives to keep all jarring elements (dramatic twists, gimmicky angles or erudite centrings) from getting between, on the one hand, his actions and attitudes towards things, and, on the other, the spectator. His art is one that ever seeks the greatest simplicity,[30] which is to say that he does not explicitly pose himself problems of expression, but that he is spontaneously creative. One must nevertheless not lose sight of the important role played by composition in his films, composition taking the form of "geometrisation"[31] both as concerns the individual and the film in its entirety, in its construction. It is this acute sense of composition. which, in the long run, is responsible for the simplicity and the limpidity of the positioning of Keaton in cinematic space and time.

No need to make a fuss. The "virtuosity" of Welles, Resnais, Ophüls etc. is perfectly legitimate and laudable; but Welles-like, Resnais-like or Ophüls-like virtuosity, pure affectations of style corresponding neither to the director's personality nor to what he has to say — form without content — are perfectly contemptible. By wanting too hard to "express oneself", one expresses nothing; one merely gives vent to empty noise.

Keaton (and Chaplin) gives us the example of a director's style of

---

[30] Philippe Demun seems to be of our opinion, since he writes: " . . . Keaton's prime quality is his strangeness, and he must let nothing enter that links him to the normal, be these things dramatic twists or mere useless explanations through the *mise-en-scène*. In his combat with the world, there is no place for a referee." (op. cit., *Contre-Champ*, no. 3).

[31] What's more, he often explained this himself, cf. the following text, transcribed from *Bifur*, on rhythm: "All gags are drawn from laws of space and time. Using them as we would use living characters, we make them advance according to the needs of the particular scene, and make them adjust to our pace. A good comic scene is often the result of more mathematical calculations than a textbook on mechanics." (Published in *Bifur*, no. 4, December 1929, and reproduced in *Contre-Champ*, no. 3, May 1962).

absolute simplicity which is, however, perfectly original and perfectly necessary.

It is the luminous simplicity of his *mise-en-scène* that makes Keaton modern, that puts him in a class with Griffith as one of the greatest artists the cinema has known. "His characters' travels can be discussed and wondered at like Orson Welles's ceilings and Eisenstein's and Murnau's objects and horizons"[32].

Keaton's direction distinguishes itself by rejecting most of that which is said to be the stuff of direction.

But let us not be deluded into believing that this "simple" direction is insignificant. As we have already seen, its very limpidity presupposes consummate artistry and, consequently, great expressive richness. His contempt for all that is traditionally called aesthetic enables Keaton to define an aesthetic.

Indeed, if Keaton seems to comply with Lenin's dictum that "ethics are the aesthetics of the future", the ethics that emerge from his films are nothing other than his activity in the world. There is no doubt that Keaton is a film-maker[33]; he is also a total creator, the only difference between him and his illustrious *confrères* being that while they have a "world vision", he has a "world action". His expressive perfection therefore consists first of all in putting forth this "world action."

Buster Keaton's cinema is a cinema "of facts and results ... in magistral opposition to all 'thinking' cinema, other adjectives of which must be dispensed with: psychological, social, divine, etc."[34]

But this "world action" — the direction of which requires a tre-

---

[32] André Martin, op. cit. p. 30.

[33] He is also a total film-maker, as he is a total athlete, since he is at the same time director, actor scenarist and editor.

[34] André Martin, op. cit., p. 26.

mendous physical discipline, a keen visual eye, a sense of choreography and an ability to dominate cinematic space by making the body and its very admirable movements fit into space perfectly — this "world action" is not gratuitous; it is not a game; it is full of ethical meaning.

For, as Keaton said: "Because I find it easy to scratch my left ear with my toe you may think me incapable of having opinions on poetry or music. But after all, learning how to scratch your ear with a toe requires stong muscular discipline, and every discipline implies another, cerebral discipline"[35].

All action, inasmuch as it brings about results and reflects a certain way of viewing things, is based on reason and has itself a certain meaning; this meaning is expressed in the *form* that the action takes; and because an action does not proclaim its intentions it does not mean that they are not inherent in the action. And that is what Buster Keaton's attitude in the world implies — that attitude which, in the comic film, takes the form of the gag — and what remains to be examined.

But first, let's look at another, closely related problem, the resolution of which usually serves to define the artist's sensitivity and confer what is known as "human value" on his work. This problem is the moral backdrop against which Keaton's pantomime takes place; it answers the question "What lesson can be drawn from this?" and concerns the "values" he puts in action, the things he condones, the things he condemns.

[35] Interview in *Bifur* no. 4, December 1929 and reproduced in *Contre-Champ*, no. 3, May 1962

4. A Backdrop Without Values

CRITICS share in common, and stubbornly adhere to, the contention that "the comic is never more profound and more admirable than when he is expressing intentions which are, however, perfectly expressible by other means"[1].

It is this contention that has led most of them to babble about the "profound humanity" of the great comics and, in Keaton's case, either by studying only his scenarios[2] or by singling out some particular characteristic as being his sole identifying one (his impassivity, his seeming "insensitivity", his seeming "fatalistic stoicism", his manner of fitting into our mechanised world, his "loneliness" etc.) to end up inevitably by making of him the eternal reincarnation of "man's despair", of "man's desperate lucidity" and "fatal tranquillity" in the face of destiny, etc. . . .

This contention (Chaplin is no doubt at the source of it) is usually presented in the most cloyingly tearful form.[3] Nor is a taste for it limited to those illiterate bumpkins who scribble in provincial gossip-sheets or those twopenny hacks who fill up space in big city rags; our most eminent cinema historians, the vanguard of our "serious" cinema critics, cannot forego their penchant (unconscious or no) for this delectable masochism. From *Télérama* to *Les Lettres Françaises*, from Henri Agel to Georges Sadoul, from *Positif* to

[1] J. P. Coursodon, "B. K. Le Conquérant Solitaire", *Cinéma* 58, no. 30, September-October 1958, p. 32.

[2] And doing so moreover in a fragmentary manner.

[3] Chaplin is less responsible for this than those who try to explain him away, for Chaplin is the first victim of this dripping sentimentality which has all but drowned all his work. Luckily his work itself remains intact, and stands up for itself, despite certain unfortunate Chaplinesque exaggerations which seem to call for this kind of interpretation.

Cahiers du Cinéma, each tries to race the other to the end of this cul-de-sac.

Fortunately there exist people like André Martin and J. P. Coursodon, real "Keatonites" who have resisted and reacted against these tendentious formulae (and were the first to do so, too).

"Avoiding personal motives, biographical determination and polemic relations with the world (contempt for theology, aggressive satire, melancholic withdrawal, social criticism) Keaton has succeeded better than all others in avoiding those allegorical, parabolic, quasi-political, social and humanist traps"[4].

"For the past thirty years, whenever the subject of Keaton has come up, talk has immediately reverted to the drama of the individual in a struggle to the death with objects and an inhumanly mechanised universe, to the point where Keaton tends to become a more highly specialised sub-Chaplin. It must be admitted, however, that our man does not facilitate things for those who would lead him down this so spiritually seductive path"[5].

This healthy reaction is, of course, admirable; but there is a danger; in one's struggle to right false interpretations, one can go to extremes and arrive at equally false interpretations of another kind. For example, Coursodon finds himself talking in terms of "pure comedy", and such talk is just as suspect as talk of "human comedy": "And *that* is what one admires in Chaplin when, in *Modern Times*, he calls our attention to problems *beyond the scope of comedy* (our italics) by giving an *illustration* of these problems which is nothing more than that. It was the politico-socio-economic background that made us laugh at the eating machine or the way he continued tightening bolts mechanically even after leaving the fac-

---

[4] A. Martin, op. cit., *Cahiers du Cinéma*, no. 86, pp. 24 and 29.

[5] J. P. Coursodon, op. cit., *Cinéma* 58, no. 30, p. 32.

tory, for the *purely comic* force (our italics) of these things is far from exceptional." ... "One thing is certain: Keaton never claims to give us food for thought, and in a similar situation his kind of comedy suffices unto itself"[6].

There is no such thing as a "purely comic force"; all comedy is built on certain facts and develops in a certain climate of sensitivity and in a definite ideological context[7]; whether or not it means to be so, laughter is never "pure"; it is rife with meaning.

It is a much more serious matter when Coursodon starts talking about "problems beyond the scope of comedy". Here he is treading on dangerous, Bergsonian ground and, like Bergson, ends up by implying a separation between comedy and life.[8] Comedy is not a domain unto itself like pure mathematics, physics or cooking.[9] Comedy is an attitude towards life, a particular attitude, to be sure, but an attitude which is taken towards all aspects of life. If, as Coursodon says, nothing can be gained by "translating *Das Kapital* into slapstick"[10] that is because the philosophical attitude and the comic attitude have nothing in common. Which is not to say that a kind of comic equivalent of *Das Kapital* is not possible; it might be extremely funny, but it would have no philosophical value. In short, the work might reveal that the system known as capitalism ought to be destroyed rather than perpetuated, but would have no demon-

---

[6] J. P. Coursodon, op. cit., pp. 32-33.

[7] Coursodon's defence reaction is itself proof of this.

[8] A very sad state of affairs for a slapstick adept.

[9] Of course physics, mathematics and cooking can be *applied* to life; in fact they only have meaning for us when they are, but comedy is an attitude that depends on life for its very existence.

[10] One cannot help remarking Coursodon's curious association of ideas: why in the devil's name must he invoke Marx after having denounced a confusionist vision of mechanisation which in that of the part of *Modern Times* mentioned above, and which has absolutely nothing to do with the Marxist conception of mechanisation?

stratively philosophical value as an analysis of the mechanics of the system.[11]

In other words, the film *Das Kapital* would have meaning inasmuch as the book *Das Kapital* already exists and could serve as a guide to it: but the film itself would explain nothing; at the very most it would demonstrate something. For all that, there's no reason why the film should *want* to mean anything.

In any event, Coursodon soon rejects this opinion which is just as false as the opinions he's been denouncing, and, with a more precise explanation, removes the air of tendentiousness from his earlier formula: "Keaton does not choose subjects for their satirical possibilities, but should such possibilities present themselves, he makes the most of them. In *The General* his successive costume changes are just one of his ways of showing the total absurdity of war, and it takes no conspiratorial wink to make us appreciate the criminal stupidity of generals who command trains to cross bridges too frail to bear their weight"[12]. And, once again referring to Keaton's adventures with mechanical objects, Coursodon attributes a "meaning" to Keaton's work, and puts forth a view which we come close to subscribing to: " . . . Let us admit that far from being lost in and overwhelmed by a world of machines, Keaton shows proof of dexterity, composure, a mechanical taste and a technological aptitude, and is thus able to control the most precarious situations . . . Let us admit our admiration for his astonishing ability to assimilate and adjust, and stop seeing in his "poems" on the

[11] On the other hand, one might be able to envisage a kind of "slapstick" review of Keaton's films. This might be side-splitting but would have no critical value. Criticism, which tries to take a total view of a work while giving it a meaning and a dimension, takes more of a philosophical attitude to life than a "slapstick" one (alas).

[12] J. P. Coursodon, op. cit., p. 33.

relations between men and matter, a plea for the maladjusted"[13].

Our analysis of Coursodon's article gives us the opportunity to look into one particular aspect of Keaton's comedy which one might call his "amorality", or ,in other words, his way of approaching situations with no intention of illustrating any preconceived ideas, as well as a certain attitude to adopt with respect to this point. For what is important is Keaton's *way* of approaching situations, not the situations themselves. All situations have, of necessity, moral or social implications. What Keaton shows us first and foremost, is that he has no moraliser hidden beneath his comic exterior.

All ideas of "pure" and "impure" comedy aside, what gives a work meaning is what makes it funny in the first place, and not what may be lurking in the background, implied but not expressed.[14] To take up once again Coursodon's remark on what critics see in comics, let us state that it is not a question of a comic being "never more profound and more admirable than when he is expressing intentions which are, however, perfectly expressible by other means" but a question of determining, not the intentions (a hardly suitable word) but rather the implications, the significance, the deeper meaning of the comic's actions. *That* is the question.

This is not to say that one must gloss over the situations in which the comic's actions take place as being of secondary importance. One must lose sight of nothing, one must take all into account, in order to determine the full significance of Keaton's work.

---

[13] J. P. Coursodon, op. cit., pp. 33-34.

It was not so much our intention above to push Coursodon's meaning to extremes as to clarify the matter for ourselves and face this question of a work's "meaning" with the maximum of honesty. We therefore felt it necessary to eliminate all trace of ambiguity. There was absolutely no personal animosity intended. Quite the contrary.

[14] Which is not to say that one must question the "essence" of comedy.

*   *   *

We have, in *Convict 13*, a perfect example of what we might call "Keaton's amorality"[15]. Keaton is about to be hung; we see the executioner strutting around, pinning on his medals, and we see Keaton himself acting a bit coquettish. Next we see the other prisoners, as enthusiastic as if they were about to witness a circus or a bullfight. A "theatre attendant" wanders through the crowd handing out sweets.

As the result of a series of unfortunate accidents the executioner fails to hang Keaton and is roundly hissed by the spectators, not because they want to save Keaton, but rather because the executioner, by bungling his job, has ruined their pleasure. Their displeasure turns into a riot and a mutiny. Keaton helps to bring the mutineers to themselves, and, in turn, becomes prison warden himself (and, why not? executioner).

Apart from the habitual turnabouts in Keaton's films, we have here a perfect example of his "amorality". Keaton spares no one. Neither the prisoners nor the executioner are particularly praiseworthy. But Keaton raises no moral question, puts his actions to the service of no established code of conduct: he acts. And all that matters is his action and its efficacity. There is no explanation as to why he is going to be hung, no question of justice or injustice. All we have is the *fact*, and the fact is that he is going to be hung.

His problem is how to get out of an unpleasant situation. He gets out of it. He takes advantage of the mutiny to join forces with the ruling forces: the cops. He becomes a cop. He does not choose to

---

[15] And not "immorality" which would be a systematic rejection of common morality and thus of moral values.

become a cop (the film is not a defence of cops). It's just that the best way to avoid being executed is to become the executioner, the cop. Everything depends on the uniform you wear.

Nor is it a matter of putting *moral relativity* in perspective, of the uniform you wear making you black or white . . .

Keaton makes no attempt to "explain things"; he merely takes the most efficacious role in regard to the given situation. And thus he gives us an example of the American form of the "survival of the fittest", of the American success-mystique. In the struggle for success anything goes; but above all, Keaton's amorality shows superficial morality up for what it is, the mere outer forms of morality with the deeper meanings lost. By posing himself no moral questions in a world that calls itself moral, his amoral success makes this pseudo-morality absurd. For, if he doesn't inform us why he is going to be hung (no moral cause) he nevertheless does shows us that a man is going to be hung (implication: morality) and, consequently, by turning the mechanisms of this hanging into an opportunity for genuine opportunism (and doing so brilliantly) he also makes mincemeat of the presumed moral foundations of these actions.

It is therefore uniquely in terms of his action that Keaton resolves upon a course to be taken; and if this action implies moral judgment or enlightenment, such is uniquely with respect to the conditions which permit its effectiveness.

Keaton's amorality, similarly applied, can be found in *Cops*.

His amorality lies in the fact that he *accepts everything* without any preconceived ideas. There's no denying that he lights his cigarette with an anarchist's bomb; nor does he divert the bomb from its original target since he, in turn, throws it back into the midst of the crowd of cops. By doing so he sparks their anger; they, of course, blindly consider him to be an anarchist, whereas he is

83

entirely oblivious to moral problems and, in short, couldn't care less.

Keaton is not a cop hater; but — comically and normally — cops represent blind repression, and Keaton cannot help being aware of that[16]. If there seems to be a latent value judgment made in regard to the police in his films, this is all due solely to "realism".

In *Cameraman*, deep in a melancholy revery, Keaton comes up against a policeman with whom he has had some run-ins already. This immediately brings him to his senses, and he dashes off. Keaton might say: "When I see a cop, I run!" The result would be a question of habit, not an intentional moral judgment. Keaton has learnt that in such cases the best thing to do is "to make oneself scarce".

When, in *The Saphead*, after all the stockholders in the New York Stock Exchange have trampled on his hat and Keaton starts trampling on *their* hats, his act is not one of revenge, is not a moral judgment on the stockmarket world and its practices, and less, still, on the society that engenders it; but, rather, it is an attempt on his part to play by the rules of the game; hat trampling seems to be the thing to do in the Stock Exchange if one wants to get ahead.

None of which stops him from showing pitilessly, in a manner worthy of von Stroheim, the mores of this world, and doing so better than if such had been his intention.

*   *   *

Keaton's energy and consequent use of force have nothing to do with any taste for violence on his part. Quite the contrary!

---

[16] Note that Keaton has no monopoly on this "anti-cop" complex which appeared in much of the early comic cinema; getting the best of cops was, with the Keystone Cops, one of the surest sources of laughter — and was all done in good fun.

Force does not represent a value for Keaton. It is merely that his way through the world inevitably brings him up against violence and force. His "moral" reaction to violence and force in general is analogous to his "moral" reaction to "cops". Besides, under the circumstances, the aforesaid policemen only represent a particular avatar of blind force, namely violence. Most of his work reflects a kind of aversion to violence.

When there is no other way out he meets force with force, but with resignation and a kind of haughty delicacy. His way of coshing people is nothing short of gentlemanly, making a slight apologetic bow as he brings the club down, bending his torso in a graceful and, at the same time, terribly efficient homage. Keaton is always elegant, even when he's braining people.

Other examples of his stunning use of his body[17] are to be found in *Paleface* and *The General*, in the former when he uses the post to which he is tied to knock out the Indian making a pyre at his feet, and in the latter when he clobbers two Northern sentries in a row, especially the second of the two, with the butt of the rifle he has secured from the first, by a simple flexing of the torso. By the same token, it's with a kind of lightly hesitant, delicate benevolence that he drops coconuts on the heads of the savage natives in *The Navigator*.

Keaton's aversion to handling guns is also noteworthy. He doesn't like to provoke people; he doesn't like to brandish guns under people's noses, he prefers merely to "inform" his adversaries that he has a gun, but he almost hides the instrument (cf. *The General*, when Keaton captures the Northern officer who only comes to, after the battle on Rock River, in Keaton's train — and, also,

---

[17] Which remains, no matter how violent the situation and the act, perfectly poised and perfectly composed.

Paleface, when one of the oil bandits tries to escape and Keaton, following him on all fours, taps him on the shoulder and shows him the gun he is holding).

In *Paleface*, too, Keaton hesitates to threaten the oilmen who refuse to return the property deed they have stolen from the Indians. It's with a certain regret that, to the bandits' horror, he nods to the Sioux to begin their scalp dance. Keaton is firm but dislikes threats, and always seems to find it deplorable that things must come to such a pass.

In *Battling Butler*, a film in which he must really confront violence and brute force head on, Keaton does so with the utmost reluctance and only for love. During his first training bout he refuses to hit his opponent. Pummelled, beaten, mercilessly flung about, when at last he does strike a few blows he seems to apologise for them, to regret that he has been reduced to them, but after all he can't let so untenable a situation go on forever, and besides, he does want to please his trainer who wants him to fight. But punching terrorises him almost as much as being punched.

Love is what drives him most of the time towards brutality and force. And only when he realises that force represents a value for others does he respond to it. He suffers at the start from a kind of "muscle complex".

In *The General* the recruiting officer, considering him more useful as a mechanic than a soldier, rejects him; extremely upset[18], Keaton sees the recruiting officer give the man behind him his draft papers, and admires the man's size and strength; then he sees another volunteer who appears to be no smaller nor larger than himself; he runs to this man and starts feeling his muscles, comparing them to his own.

[18] His success in love will depend on his being a soldier and a hero.

86

But for Keaton violence is not the goal of physical excellence and self-accomplishment. He clearly prefers athletic feats, not merely in *College* where he goes out for almost all sports: baseball, gymnastics, sculling, etc., but in many of his other films as well.

When called upon to come to the aid of a lady (which almost always gives him the opportunity to perform physical wonders) he runs, he flies, he braves the elements, etc., but he rarely directs his energy to destructive ends against men. Exposed to the vengeance of hereditary enemies who quite simply want to kill him in *Our Hospitality*, it is not from these enemies that he saves his beloved, but rather from the waves and the mountain. And yet Keaton is not one for moralising on people who go in for violence. In *The Cameraman*, during a battle in the Chinese quarter, while not quite spurring the fighters on hysterically (which would be unlike him), Keaton does correct battle positions, return lost weapons and encourage the men when the battle begins to wane. But this is not so much out of love for war as out of a sense of artistry; the quality of his news-film depends on it. And what he really seems to be saying is: "If these people must fight, at least let them do so properly."

Force and power are always at the bottom of his relations with women. If not required to perform deeds of force and power to win their hearts, he must do so at least to defend them, or to defend himself from them. In *Seven Chances* a hoard of hideous old maids, of lovestruck spinsters, chases him through a church, through the city and the countryside which becomes increasingly more savage, primitive and exotic.

In the prehistoric episode from *The Three Ages*, Keaton, a slimly elegant young man, goes in quest of a woman. Coming upon a beauty nonchalantly reposing, he lies down at her side and begins to woo her. Unresponsive to Keaton's charms she rises indignantly, unbending and straightening her giant's body above his frail form.

It is a woman who is responsible for what is perhaps Keaton's most significant statement in regard to violence. In *Battling Butler*, to please the girl he loves and especially to get in good with her father and brother, two beefy fellows who would never give the girl to a puny runt, Keaton pretends, despite his better judgment, to be a champion boxer (his name is Alfred Butler, like the champion, Alfred "Battling" Butler).

It is not Keaton but the real Battling Butler who fights the crucial press-heralded match, the outcome of which makes him a kind of world champion. But after the match, the reprieve accorded Keaton having expired, the real champion decides to give the impostor a lesson. He starts knocking poor Keaton about, playing with him like a cat with a half-dead mouse, determined to break every bone in his body. And that is when Sally O'Neill appears on the dressing-room threshold. Keaton, till now a toy in the boxer's fists, little by little begins defending himself; he resists and, finally, drawing on a hitherto unsuspected energy, lets himself go and k.o.'s the real Battling Butler.

No miracle (explicable or not) has taken place, no foreign element has been introduced to take the credit for Keaton's triumph. He owes it all to himself, to an effort of all his being, to a prodigious moral force manifesting itself in the form of physical energy.

After his victory, Keaton looks humble as ever; he preserves the same tranquil assurance, the same serene poise. Perhaps he reproaches the girl slightly for having obliged him to take such steps. If there is two-way gratitude in the last shot of *Battling Butler* (Sally's gratitude to Keaton for being so valorously noble and Keaton's gratitude to Sally for having given him the opportunity to surpass himself) there is also mute reproach for this barbarous act to which

At right:
THE NAVIGATOR

Below: GO WEST.

he has been obliged to abandon himself.

And this reproach is all the more effective because it is the judgment not of a weakling and a victim, but of a man who, weak and victimised, has triumphed, and who considers his victory degrading, not ennobling.

But let us not be deluded into believing that the final shot of *Battling Butler* is one of despair. No matter what the proponents of "Keatonian despair" may say, Keaton himself is not even implying that, in the long run, no matter what one struggles for here on earth, no matter what one fights for, all is nought but degradation leaving a bitter taste in the mouth.

Keaton, opposed to brute force, finds in his moral energy the means to vanquish it on its own terrain. Which is to say that for Keaton, in the end, the force and moral nobility[19] he incarnates are *factually* more effective than violence, and not that ideals "here below" will always come up against "necessity": that, sooner or later, one must abandon one's purity or perish, beaten by the world's ignominy. If Keaton triumphs over brute force on its own terrain, this is not because he himself has become a brute. Far from it; the tranquil energy he represents is superior to brute force *only because* it can emerge triumphant.

Women, therefore, bring out Keaton's force and energy. What, then, are his relations with women?

VALOROUS LOVE?

(Note on Buster Keaton and Women)
Women are usually at the root of those performances in which

[19] In all its poetic forms.

Keaton surpasses himself so extraordinarily.

Just as it has been said that Keaton has no intention of addressing a "message of general interest"[20], it has been said that Keaton "doesn't love". "If he is amorous in all his films, his love is tepid and comes more of habit than conviction"[21].

Such critics are confusing *love* with *sentimentality*. For indeed, when it comes to billing and cooing, Keaton certainly does show little conviction. He loses his footing in sentimentality and drowns in rose water.

Keaton, for whom the woman serves as an impetus to show what he can do, to surpass himself, and therefore to show that he loves, is ill at ease when it comes to wooing a girl in a normal fashion. When he must win her with well-phrased compliments and facile gallantry *(The Cameraman, College, Sherlock Junior, Seven Chances, The Navigator)* he always loses out to others. When he must court her on a sofa with flowers *(The Navigator)* or with bonbons *(Sherlock Junior)* or with love letters *(Seven Chances)* or with simple declarations and customary gallantries *(The Cameraman, College,* the portrait in *The General,* etc.) he's a dismal flop. But when he must work wonders to woo and win her, *then* he is in his element. Only put him in a storm-tossed ship and you'll see if he knows how to woo a woman or not.

In *The Navigator*, he is — beneath his seemingly cold exterior — taken by so great an exaltation for the girl he loves, that he seeks the grandiose. He would fly through space to get to her, but is reduced to crossing the street in his huge limousine, performing a graceful but limited U-turn which seems to call for wider flights.

---

[20] Always as a reaction to that literature consecrated to Chaplin, and which would strive to place Keaton in the realm of pure comedy.

[21] J. P. Coursodon, op. cit., *Cinema* 58, no. 30, p. 34.

(Here, too, it's the form Keaton's act, his gag, takes — its positioning in space — which gives us its meaning, a meaning more significant than the act itself)[22].

In the same token, when he must declare his love to a girl on a garden swing, according to the rules, he flounders; but when he must woo her while striving to hold himself up before a table which is sinking in the earth *(Battling Butler)*, he does so marvellously.

Similarly, he is at a disadvantage when it comes to "taking out" the girl he loves *(The Cameraman)*. At the swimming pool he more or less manages to make a good impression; he is, after all, in his element there, and can shine. But when it comes to making small talk and driving her home, Keaton finds himself in the dickey seat, in the rain, while his rival scores points.

Keaton is not "tepid". Quite the contrary. It's just that he dislikes cramped banality; he spices things. When, in *Sherlock Junior*, he overturns the box of chocolates to show the price, this is not an intentionally provocative act. But he is like a child, proud and happy to show the value of the beautiful gift he has given. For Keaton the gesture does not count so much as the intensity of the gesture, and in this case the intensity of the gesture is given by the price sticker.

Let this act help him to break the bonds of cramped banality and Keaton will be completely prepared to give himself over to traditional billing and cooing.

As, for instance, the two-year kiss which ends *The Paleface*. Two

[22] This proves that in the end Keaton is never satisfied with comfort. He may be used to it, but he never makes a value of it. When everything seems too comfortable at the start, he puts all sorts of obstacles in his way (as, for instance, the first part of *The Navigator* or the first part of *Battling Butler* when, as the son of an upper-class family, Keaton finds himself in the grip of an ultra-perfected camping equipment). Only later will he have to fend for himself and utilise a maximum of energy and ingenuity (the fight in *Battling Butler*, the domestication scene in *The Navigator*.) Keaton does not succeed on his social position but on his personal merits, which have nothing to do with any kind of domesticity.

years is a long time for a kiss to last; but above all, one has the impression that Keaton sustained it for two years because the position in which he found himself with the young Indian maiden was of such visual beauty, was so perfectly placed in space[23], that two years seemed a suitable duration for it.

Keaton is ever ready to "call on" the girl he loves, to throw his love-sick heart at her feet[24], if to do so he must make a mockery of distance and present himself before her at the end of an incredible run, hardly breathless, excusing himself for being slightly late, although she has just finished asking him to come on the telephone. *(The Cameraman)*[25].

It is therefore unfair to say that Keaton does not love. Considering the prodigies he performs for the sake of women, it's hard not to call the feeling that inspires these prodigies love. As a matter of fact, Keaton is the only comic hero who succeeds in giving real scope to his love. Alone in the comic cinema where sexuality plays almost no role to speak of[26] and where most manifestations of love are reduced to feeble attempts at sentimental billing and cooing, Keaton stands out not as a platonic but rather as a courtly lover.

Indeed, apart from occasional mishaps with some diabolical Venus[27], Keaton is a gallant knight. No one would dream of denying this; the remarkable feats that he performs to win, protect or save

[23] In that famous oblique position which his sweetheart shares with him here.

[24] Actions which, in themselves, hardly appeal to him.

[25] In this same film, too, as love-struck as any matinee idol, he is fully prepared to wait to receive a bitchy telephone call, if waiting will enable him to do wonders on the building staircase.

[26] "There is no sex, no passion, for the comic actor. When a woman kissed me I became a father to her. I wanted to protect her for the rest of her life". (Statement made by Keaton to the interviewer for *Cahiers du Cinéma*, no. 86, August 1958, p. 29, photo caption).
If Keaton has a tendency towards platonic love (here "paternal") he does not differ in that from all other cinema comics, with the possible exception of Langdon who, it seems, is repressed, and lets it be seen.

[27] Cf. above.

his lady, constitute the principal dramatic springboard of almost all his films.

Unlike Chaplin who, if he doesn't win his lady's heart by out-witting the villain or by a stroke of luck, is loved for his weakness itself, Keaton wins *his* lady's heart by his very real triumph. It is his force and his courage which overcomes his timidity and assures Keaton his greatest success.

At the end of the Roman episode of *The Three Ages*, Keaton, a leaping, flying Douglas Fairbanks-type avenger, tears his lady from the clutches of the "villains" and metes them out a severe but well-merited punishment.

Love brings out Keaton's matchless ingenuity and indefatigable energy, makes him perform marvellous visual and physical feats, and become a veritable hero *(The General)*.

Love enables Keaton to bring a liner gone berserk under control *(The Navigator)*.

Love makes him master of a tempest and enables him to save a ship, its owner and his daughter from the storm *(Steamboat Bill Junior)*.

Love makes him play the indomitable detective *(Sherlock Junior)*.

Love makes him the most fantastic news reporter ever seen, makes him direct a street battle and save his girl from the diabolical machi-nations of a maddened outboard motorboat and a certain death by drowning *(The Cameraman)*.

Love enables him to save his girl, at the last moment, from the crashing falls of a mute Niagara *(Our Hospitality)*.

Love makes him break more sports records than any athlete has ever broken *(College)*.

And so on.

When we say that love makes Keaton perform the countless

incredible feats that lard his films and show him in all his visual beauty, we do not mean to say that love is necessarily, in its crudest form, the direct cause of what drives him to perform these feats. Another cause that is not love may put him in a position to perform them (in *The Navigator*, it is chance). But inasmuch as these deeds are always what makes the girl (who has hitherto usually repulsed his advances) recompense him, love profoundly determines Keaton's actions in the second stage.

The feats performed by Keaton when in love owe nothing to chance. He alone is responsible for them. In *College*, for instance, sheer strength of will, fed by love, permits him to lead his sculling team to victory, to achieve the final turnabout, effect his astounding hurdle race and become the best athlete in the college. And this is what differentiates him from all other comics.

The finest example of Keaton's manner of surpassing himself for the sake of love is obviously the one already given in *Battling Butler* when, first a toy in the violent and expert hands of the professional boxer, Keaton manages to turn the situation about and knock the boxer out, purely by calling up his own untapped forces. The slow development of the change in Keaton, *all of which takes place before our eyes*, is properly admirable. In a similar situation Chaplin would have slipped a horseshoe into his boxing glove, or clumsily bumped up against something which would cause a heavy weight to fall on his adversary's head.

For Keaton the woman is obviously therefore a sort of catalyst, *an opportunity for him to surpass himself*. It is the woman who reveals him to himself, who enables him to effect the remarkable physical, athletic, dynamic, choreographic and visual self-accomplishment we spoke of earlier in this book, all of which is the sign of a sort of moral ascendancy.

Inasmuch as love makes him surpass himself and forget himself, makes him open to the world and produces in him a self-accomplishment on a higher level, love for Keaton has Éluardian overtones, the only difference being that for Éluard, love is a question of reciprocal self-surpassing, and love opens a man to others.

In Keaton's films, as has often been stressed[28], love is not usually a reciprocal matter. Women often display a certain indifference towards him (for which reason he is led to surpass himself). Nor are they always and immediately grateful for what he does for them; at times, in fact, relations between Keaton and his girls are rather strained. The girl in *The Navigator* shows a certain ungraciousness; she even does him some nasty turns, as, for instance, when she obliges him to put on a diving suit and repair the propeller. When Annabelle's foot gets caught in a trap in *The General*, Keaton gets it out; but in so doing his own foot, as well as a hand, gets caught in it; the furious girl is completely indifferent to poor Keaton's plight.

But the girl he chooses always ends by loving him. Keaton is not "unlucky in love". It may take time to make the girl love him, and she may love him less passionately than he loves her, but she will love him eventually nevertheless.

The trials he imposes on himself to "merit" his lady are of the same nature as those imposed on knights in the time of courtly love. Keaton, too, engages in tournaments to win his lady, but his tournaments are of a slightly special nature, for in them he jousts with the whole world.

But the gallant knight, having won his lady's heart at last, can allow himself to indulge in billing and cooing. Knights, even fearless fighting knights, are adept at turning pretty phrases. But to turn

[28] For the sake of drawing hasty conclusions.

these phrases without first fighting for the right to turn them is meaningless for Keaton. Because he has been accepted by the girl does not mean that he can sink back into a dull routine. In *Battling Butler*, only after Keaton has wed Sally O'Neill does he really surpass himself. Besides which, and unlike the knights of old, Keaton does not really consider the woman to be his goal, to be an end in herself; the woman is above all a means for him to surpass himself.

Surpassing himself constitutes the very *form* his love takes. His proving himself is homage to the lady. Displaying his possibilities is not merely the means to win the lady's favours; the display itself is the very incarnation of his love.

Many have held that Keaton, contrary to appearances, does not love women because they introduce disorder into his ordered universe. This false supposition rests on a false appreciation of the very nature of Keaton's character. If Keaton puts the world in order, this is not because he's seeking bourgeois comfort; he is not the mythical incarnation of the little tinkerer who always gets by. Such a conception requires that Keaton be an inhibited little person closed in on himself. But the ultimate goal of his activity is not to secure for himself a tranquil corner of the universe, well protected against the unforeseen; and to want to see his actions as such is to want to see in him a stoic experiencing life fatalistically as he struggles to survive.

Now, we have seen that Keaton is concentration open to the world. The "poetic" way he handles objects bears witness to that. His very readiness to throw himself into the most dangerous adventures for the sake of a woman is only one more indication of his openness to receive and accept all that calls to him.

And love, which gives him the opportunity to accomplish himself supremely, shows us again how open he is to the world. At the end of *The Cameraman* we see Keaton, led along by the girl he has won at last and with whom he shall at last taste happiness (thereby fulfilling the logic of his love) accept the cheers of a crowd, cheers intended for Lindbergh but which Keaton has earned as much as the aviator, if not more.

And thus we see that Keaton's luck in love, far from cutting him off from the world, shows how capable he is of assimilating and openly responding to the call of life and of doing so masterfully.

*   *   *

One last example will enable us to sum up all we have said with respect to the form Keaton's love takes, his openness to the world and the expressiveness of his direction considered as the physical positioning of his action.

At the end of *The General*, seated on the piston of his locomotive with Annabelle, now his fiancée, Keaton prepares to kiss her. Seated to her left, he holds her by the shoulders with his right arm, and hugs her with his left arm in front. At this moment a soldier leaves a tent and passes in front of the couple, going in the direction of the wash-house. Keaton, just become an officer, is obliged to answer the soldier's salute and to do so must free his right arm and turn his body slightly. The disturbance over, Keaton returns to his original position and prepares to kiss the girl. Another soldier, then a third, then a fourth and finally the whole regiment leave the tents for the wash-house. Seeing this, Keaton rises and seats himself on the girl's right. He now puts his left arm around her shoulders and, with his right arm free, in perfect compliance with military protocol, he salutes the passing soldiers and kisses Annabelle at the same time.

Let us first admire the way this burlesque gag is carried to perfection, and its *turnabout*.[29] The premises develop slowly before our eyes until, suddenly, the solution shoots up like a plant in accelerated motion and bursts into flower, thereby corresponding perfectly to a certain definition of the gag.[30]

An ordinary gag would have ended with the departure of all the soldiers. The hero would have gone off tearing his hair, and the audience would have burst out laughing. The audience does, in fact, laugh at that moment in Keaton's gag, but it laughs doubly[31] at the admirable final solution.

The spectator's inability to predict what was going to happen leaves him bewildered by and marvelling at Keaton's foresight and solution. All of which provoke cries of "Marvellous!" "Genius!" "Wonderful!" and the laughter which certifies the gag's perfection.[32]

This gag proves first of all that Keaton is ever ready to let himself be amorous when an amorous act has an athletic side to it; when, far from bringing him some lazy comfort, it pushes him to surpass and "sur-adjust" himself; and, too, it gives him the opportunity to display his ingenuity and his adjustment faculties to the utmost, thereby increasing the fervour of his kiss.

The kiss is therefore not merely an expression of himself, but of

---

[29] We shall return to this point later.

[30] "Though some may consider a gag to be anything humorous, others reserve this term to designate a particular visual form the finest examples of which are enshrined in works of that golden silent era ... for there is certainly an almost classical form which begins and develops in a manner calculated to prolong a visual situation, and then, swinging suddenly, gives it a new meaning and an unsuspected value." (A. Martin, "Un Cinéma fini", *Cinéma 60*, no. 49, August-September 1960, p. 3 and p. 97).

"Every gag can be broken down into three parts: (1) a situation. (2) a particular action within this situation. (3) the completion of this action which is at the same time both logical and preposterous." (F. Mars, "Autopsie du gag," I. *Cahiers du Cinéma*, no. 113, November 1960, p. 25).

[31] And more still.

[32] The order is evidently reversed: the cries of appreciation only come when the laughter is over.

his intelligence, subtlety and power of adjustment as well. And the remarkable self-accomplishment that the kiss represents incarnates more a reflection of the homage he pays his lady than a mere contact of his loving lips with hers.

Second, this gag is evidence that Keaton never refuses any solicitation, any call from the world. It is evidence of his poly-adjustment. The normal attitude in a similar situation would be to flee to a quiet spot, there to love his lady in peace. But Keaton does not give way; he does not shirk a difficulty. He can rise to any situation, and he therefore kisses the girl and salutes the troops *at the same time*.

Thirdly, this gag is evidence that the solution is always a question of the *mise-en-scène*. The solution is resolved by his body's adjustment to a new positioning, for this solution, this adjustment, this form that his action takes, is always expressed in *physical* terms and in spatial relations.

*　　*　　*

If the study of certain "values" inherent in Keaton's work has given us some information on what gives his behaviour coherence, on his "world action", it is clear that no study can explain this world action to us, nor give us the key to it.

Indeed, Keaton's "amorality", his "horror of the mechanised world"[33], his particular conception of love, his open attitude towards the world, his "poetic use of things"[34] for example — none of these things can give a meaning to his work for the simple reason that it

[33] Some have tried to find this in Keaton's films. We shall have ample opportunity to discuss this matter in our final chapter. Till then, we shall keep silent.

[34] Keaton's comedy is indeed profoundly poetic. As everyone knows, the only true poetry is involuntary. When an art form other than that which bears the name "poetry" rises to poetic heights, this is not because poetry was its goal. Poetry is the result of a certain way of envisaging the world (that goes without saying); it can in no way represent a principle of action.

is not these things *which make him act*. They are rather the conditions of his action — or what results from it — not the basis for this action.

Love[35] (and the openness to the world which it presupposes), though it seems effectively to represent a value for Keaton and, crystallising, can, to a certain extent, reflect and reveal the ethic expressed and incarnated in Keaton's action with respect to the world, can in no way make us aware of this action itself, or of its meaning.

It is therefore clear that the significance of Keaton's "world action" can only be found in this action itself.

And the final gag in *The General* indicates that Keaton's action, such as we have seen it at work, is situated nowhere else than in the gag itself, and that the gag alone can give us the reasons for Keaton's action as applied to beings and things.

The gag is the form that Keaton's attitude takes in regard to the world; consequently, the study of Keaton's "world action" can be nothing but the study of the structure of the gag in his films (which only makes sense — that's the least one can say — when speaking of a comic creator)[36].

---

[35] In the Keaton sense of the world, as discussed above.

[36] Q.E.D. A comic's fundamental attitude towards the world is expressed in the gag and not in extraneous elements which are only its support, conditions or reflection. This does not mean that an appreciation of Keaton rests solely on a study of the gag in his films. On the contrary, we must never lose sight of all we have learned so far about Keaton.

If the gag, in its proper structure, is the first expression of the meaning of Keaton's work (and its essential aesthetic form, inasmuch as it is related to a particular aesthetic *genre*, comedy) it is not the sole determinant, and the other aspects of Keaton's work contribute to define its breadth. The different elements of a piece of work engender one another reciprocally, giving a unity to the whole; and any analysis striving for a bare modicum of objectivity must attempt to synthesise all the different elements which serve to make up a work, and not consider each separately, in a fixed and closed manner.

5. The Gag

"A gag, like a film, is found in what is latent in the processed reel."

Louis Terrence Cop

K EATON'S action manifests itself in the use of objects. We are using object here in the fullest sense of the word; the object may be a situation that Keaton must master, the situation itself being the relation between several objects (as was the case in the final gag in *The General*). In every situation the problem presents itself to Keaton in the form of a good distribution and a proper organisation of things in space.[1]

In this sense human beings may well be considered objects[2] against which he must position himself and which he must put in order.

In the handling of objects Keaton displays his talents for organisation, geometrization, adjustment, and physical and poetic mastery of things; in a word, all that constitutes his manner of adjusting to the world, his manner of being, his "world action".

The form that this handling takes is the gag. If Keaton's most important dealings are with real objects (mechanical or other), and if these objects are to constitute the principle subject of this study, let us nevertheless not forget[3] that the Keaton gag can very well be expressed in the form of a confrontation with nature resolved in his perfect positioning in space. In such cases laughter is derived from the organisation of spatial lines and of Keaton's body in the spatial framework. In that respect, the largest "object" Keaton

---

[1] Let us not forget that the gag is essentially a visual thing, even if Groucho Marx does handle the verbal gag extraordinarily well (but that's something else again).

[2] No disparaging nuance is here intended.

[3] As we had occasion to see when talking of the visual and directing aspects of Keaton's film.

uses in his gags is the world itself.

As a comic personality[4] Keaton inevitably uses objects curiously; his reaction to a situation is never an ordinary one. He handles objects either positively or negatively. For Keaton every problem is posed in terms of success and failure. He is constantly seeking the form which will lead him to success (or to failure); i.e. the form which will put his way of adjustment in concrete form: which will lead to his integration or his non-integration.

At the start Keaton comes up against minor difficulties and experiences minor failures which do not put him off, or break down his courage and energy. But no matter the problem, be it a collapsible house, an electrified house, a hook that catches him or a trap that he falls into, his ingenuity, his energy, his athletic ability, his intelligent positioning, his beautiful and logical appearance in space will see him out into the clear. "Every obstacle and every difficulty finds him ready to apply an offensive strategy which constantly reveals how clever, deft, adroit, competent and indefatigable he is"[5]. And if, as in *Steamboat Bill Junior*, part of a wall falls in, Keaton always manages to be standing *exactly* at the window at the time[6].

When Keaton manages to extricate himself from difficulties by blunders which, rather than appearing as such, lead on to new ways of attacking the difficulties, he enjoys repeating them so as to appreciate their effectiveness all the more.

In *Cops*, using the curious directional indicator he has invented (a jointed towel-rail with a boxing glove at the end) Keaton inadver-

[4] Representing as he does an elemental experimental attitude towards life.

[5] A. Martin, "Le Mécano de la Pantomime", *Cahiers du Cinéma*, no. 86, Aug. 1958, p. 25.

[6] If flying through a window is a relatively common phenomenon, Keaton is alone in being able to do so vertically, while at the same time in a camera angle that puts him perpendicular to the window.

tently knocks down a policeman directing traffic. No sooner has the policeman risen than, turning left a second time[7], Keaton again, with the towel-rail opening like a spring, lands one on the policeman's nape and sends him sprawling.

This is not the simple repetition of a blunder as in the case in *The General* when, like a leit-motif, the Northern staff falls down every time the train comes to a stop.

The gag in *Cops* does not stem uniquely from the repetition of the action, but mainly from the perfect positioning of this repetition; things could not happen otherwise. Here Keaton's foresight is evident and indicated in the graceful curve described by his vehicle and the sureness of his trajectory, all of which will, ineluctably, lead him to repeat what he has done.

Keaton's manner of repeating the incident together with the spectator's apprehension and its corollary — surprise — enables him to define different stages of a gag.

*   *   *

In *The Navigator* Keaton and the girl frighten each other mutually. Both run like madmen through the boat and, especially, through the saloon. At one point, feeling the danger to be past, Keaton relaxes in a sheet-covered armchair. But the girl is hiding beneath the sheet and, when Keaton sits on her, her arms enfold him. Once more the two in terror run from each other. A few minutes later all seems calm again, and again Keaton passes the armchair which looks just as it did a while ago and under whose cover can be divined a human form. Keaton pauses, ponders, and sits, but: surprise of surprises! the chair topples over and the girl, horrified by the noise, surges out from behind the sofa where she has been hiding.

---

[7] To do so he must turn from his original course.

Here Keaton plays on a false repetition to increase the gag's subtlety and, seeming to play on the spectator's apprehensions, plays in fact on his surprise.

In *Paleface*, having stumbled on an Indian reservation unaware that the Indians are determined to put to death the first white man who enters, Keaton wanders dreamily about looking for butterflies. The ferocious-looking Indians slowly surround him. Meanwhile Keaton has been making his way towards the back of the field; suddenly he turns and runs in the direction of the camera, the Indians hot on his heels. And then, inexplicably, he stops short. He has caught a butterfly and now holds it in his hands.

Admirable as this gag is for its positioning and dynamic qualities, it also plays remarkably on the spectator's fears,[8] — and not on an elementary but on a very subtle level, revealing that Keaton has great confidence in the spectator's intelligence and ability to react and re-adjust rapidly.

As in the example from *The Navigator*, Keaton plays on the spectator's observational acumen as well as on his apprehension to double the comic force of a burst of action (the fall of the armchair and the simultaneous surge of the girl from behind the sofa like a jack-in-the-box).

All this is evidence of Keaton's respect for the spectator's intelligence[9]. We shall often have the opportunity to note this, particu-

---

[8] The spectator laughs because, struck by the suddenness of Keaton's take-off, he imagines him to be fleeing the Indians. By the same token, the spectator assumes (even if he lacks the time to realise this completely, inasmuch as the solution comes immediately) that Keaton's reason for stopping was the evident impossibility of escaping from the redskins.

[9] "When I started out in the movies, Fatty Arbuckle warned me: "Never forget that the mental age of the audience is never more than twelve years old." Several months later I went to him and said: "Roscoe, you'd better get that idea out of your head because anyone who goes on making films for 12 year-olds will soon be out of business. The public is always smarter than you — it has to be if it's going to enjoy what you're doing." (Buster Keaton, "Une rencontre avec Buster Keaton," J. Schmitz, *Cahiers du Cinéma*, no. 86, August 1958, p. 16.)

*SEVEN
CHANCES.*

larly when it comes to the development of gags whose premises are positioned early in the films, and whose solutions only come later on.

*   *   *

After pure and simple minor difficulties come *confusions* in objects.

In *The General*, waving a flag triumphantly, Keaton climbs on to a rock; the rock stands up. He has climbed on to a colonel's back.

In *The Saphead*, ragged by the stockholders who pull his hat over his eyes, then throw it down and stamp on it, Keaton, taking their actions for normal if curious stockmarket customs, begins himself to stamp on the stockholders' hats[10].

In *Paleface* Keaton leaps on a horse standing behind a thicket and ... goes off in the wrong direction. Two horses had been standing together head to tail, and he had leapt on the wrong horse. Rashness is the reason for this confusion.

Confusion can result from an object's failure to attain its original destination. In *The Navigator*, kept from sleep by a painting of a nasty looking sea bass, the girl throws both look and painting out the porthole. The painting gets hooked on the ship's hull and swings before Keaton's porthole. He, taking it for the decapitated head of the Loch Ness monster, is terrified.

In *Steamboat Bill Junior*, Keaton goes back to the prison from which he has just escaped, to get out of the rain.[11]

In *Cops*, trying to fit ceramic vases into a suitcase so as to keep them from breaking, Keaton jumps on the suitcase to close it, thereby breaking the large vases inside.

[10] This confusion is really the result of imitation; the gag is more complex in its implications and overall significance.

[11] But here a sort of prescience comes into account. Keaton knows that the tempest will only put off his escape temporarily, and that his hour of glory approaches.

In *The General*, in order to get his train, whose wheels are slipping, back into motion, Keaton throws some dirt on the tracks[12]. Dissatisfied with the ineffectiveness of these several grains of dust, he takes it out on the earth around him, striking it and trampling it in order to tear from it bigger clods; throughout all this he never notices that his train has disappeared.

In the same film Keaton tries to fill his water tank with a short hose. When he pulls on it to get the last length over the top of the tank, the part attached to the cistern snaps off. When he pulls on the cistern chain, the flow of water which issues directly from the cistern without passing through the hose knocks the girl down.

To repair the damage and get the girl out of her unfortunate situation, he tries re-attaching the hose to the cistern. He succeeds in this but also succeeds in soaking the girl all over again, and this time with water coming from the other end of the now-fastened hose[13].

Trying to open a moneybox in *The Cameraman*, Keaton knocks a wall over.

The contrary can happen, too. The will to succeed in a piece of action requiring many steps can make Keaton do things which seem out of keeping with the action. In *The General*, when he comes to rescue Annabelle, in order to ensure that she won't cry out when he wakes her, he throws himself on her and gags her[14].

Usually Keaton doesn't let maladroitness stop him. And if, in the end, he overcomes all difficulties, that's because he is determined to do so. More than any basic ability to succeed in a given project,

[12] One might challenge the very basis for this conduct which may work with other vehicles but not necessarily with trains.

[13] One might note here, too, the double use of the possibilities of one object, to the same end.

[14] It is obvious that this behaviour has little in common with that of romantic heroes: "Sweetheart, awake. Here am I, thy prince charming, come to save thee." This is not comparable, but certainly truer.

what drives him is his will to succeed, his determination to let nothing get in the way of his goal.

In *The General* Keaton busies himself making wood provisions by throwing logs on to the tender; but he does not throw them high enough; each time they fall back. In exasperation, he throws one log with all his might — and overshoots the tender. He starts to go after the log, although he has a pile of logs at his feet, and then, realising the stupidity of his action, stops short, and returns.

Keaton frowns on cramped conduct, both in himself and in others. In another scene in *The General* the girl is making a most conscientious effort to do the task Keaton has assigned her: to stoke the boiler. Determined as she is not to lose a splinter of wood, she drops the tiniest sprig into the furnace with the utmost delicacy; Keaton immediately hands her another sprig, smaller still, and this, too, she throws into the fire. In exasperation Keaton leaps on her and strangles her . . . before he kisses her (she had previously rejected a perfect piece of tinder under the pretext that it had a small hole in it). Nor can Keaton hide his anger when the girl, emerging from the sack, triumphantly offers him the stop-block she had taken to unhitch the train trucks and had obstinately kept with her in the sack throughout the journey.

Keaton is himself very good at making the most out of this slightly exasperating attitude which confuses the form of an action with the real action itself.

In *The General*, finding the presence of the children who follow him wherever he goes, especially when he goes to woo his lady, a bit embarrassing, Keaton rises, takes his hat, and opens the door to leave. The children go out first through the door he holds open for them; Keaton closes the door, removes his hat, and sits back down beside the girl.

111

This apparent confusion is in reality nothing but a lower form of Keaton's remarkable ability to *re-convert* objects, *assimilating* them into every situation in every way (form, function, environment) possible. Besides which, it is always obvious where the confusion ends and the positive assimilation begins.

In *The Cameraman* Keaton takes the slope of a roof for a staircase, but in treating the roof like a staircase he makes such consummate use of spatial lines, that no one would dream of calling this victory a "defeat".

Already it is evident that Keaton's way of adjusting is unique, and cannot be compared to anyone else's.

In *The Navigator* he mixes up the "environment" air with the "environment" water[15], so that one cannot tell if he's revealing an impotence in the face of things or, on the contrary, an extraordinary capacity to give "environments" new meanings. The way he invents and re-invents things is more striking than the confusions he makes between them.

Besides, after defeating a giant octopus (and doing so with his air tube cut), Keaton will calmly emerge from the water after an agonising but determined walk, and at the same time, by his frightening appearance (the diving suit) scare off the natives who have kidnapped his girl (the kidnapping was the reason for the brutal cessation of oxygen in the first place).

In *Paleface*, Keaton likens his hands tied round a pole to a ring around a finger; he frees his hands from the pole as he would remove a ring from a finger.

In *The General* he "slips on" his sabre like a pair of trousers.

---

[15] Diving down to repair the propeller, Keaton puts up a small barrier on which is written: "Attention, work in progress." and when he finishes the job, he fills a bucket with water, washes his hands, and empties the bucket.

In *Cops* there is an assimilation of a garden gate into prison bars[16]. In *The General* he empties the sack with his girl friend in it as he would a sack of potatoes; he makes bulbs explode like hand grenades.

Here *assimilation* is meant in the psychological sense of the word. An object loses its identity and is absorbed and assimilated by other objects. Keaton "drowns" his shoe in a pile of other shoes. Assimilation leads to pure and simple re-conversion, an object being cleanly transformed into another, or put to a new use.

* * *

There is a period of "becoming" when an object is midway between assimilation and re-conversion. As, for instance, Keaton's use of anachronism and latitude changes in *The Three Ages*. Attaching a meter to a Roman litter he turns it into a taxi; he puts up parking meters in front of the Forum; he equips his chariot with a spare tyre; when it snows he turns up for a race with runners in the place of his chariot wheels, and with huskies standing in for horses.

Re-conversion can remain at the point of facile transformation, as, for instance, with the rifle-oar in *Battling Butler*. (Taking his rifle by the barrel, Keaton plunges the butt into the water and rows with it). But what usually happens is a wonderful and wondrous metamorphosis of situations and things.

Sitting behind his engine, choking in the smoke from the burning truck the Northerners have left on the track, Keaton takes a huge piece of bark from the tinder pile and fans himself with it *(The General)*.

[16] Cf. Chaplin (*The Pilgrim*) who perhaps inspired this. But with Chaplin the assimilation of the bars of the railway ticket window into those of a prison is done in terms of the past, and therefore explicitly. In *Cops*, however, the assimilation is *implicit*, with respect to the future, and in terms of Keaton's appearance of mourning. The gag happens at the very beginning of the film, before he has had any run-ins with the police. It prepares one for the later difficulties.

Keaton turns a dangerous arrow into a cane, and will later turn himself into an arrow-quiver as he becomes an unharmed, serene Saint Sebastian *(Paleface)*.

By an ingenious re-conversion of his car's convertible hood into a sail, Keaton transforms his car which has fallen into the water into a small schooner *(Sherlock Junior)*.

In *College* he wrests the umbrella from an enormous dowager who wants to break it over his head[17] and metamorphoses it into a marvellous parachute, himself becoming, by the graceful slowed motion, a kind of butterfly.[18]

With a graceful rocking motion of his body, Keaton turns his diving-suited self into a boat for his lady love, an expedient which saves them both from a most unpleasant fate. The girl, rowing a paddle stolen from the natives of the Isle of X, rows them back to safety and away from the cauldron *(The Navigator)*.

In *Cops*, Keaton invents the telephone-horse. Putting earphones on the horse hitched to his cart, he transmits his orders by telephone, thereby avoiding unnecessary exercise.

In *The Cameraman* he turns the telephone *call* into concrete *presence,* inventing the carnal videophone.

Let us note here that the recurring presence of certain objects (telephones, trains, cannons, etc.) proves not merely the coherence of Keaton's world but, and above all, his immense inventive capacities. Using every object according to an imperious logic and in every way possible, he nevertheless never uses an object the same way twice. We have already established that Keaton's adjustment

---

[17] She thinks he is a Peeping Tom, spying on her as she prepares her *toilette*. Actually, his friends are bouncing him up and down in a blanket.

[18] Here already we can see how Keaton turns every possibility inherent in a situation to best advantage and develops from it a series of gags that engender the internal dynamics of the situation. Invention here is also the perfect integration into a given situation.

takes the form of an enrichment of the reality in which he participates and for which he is responsible, although the source of this enrichment is in the objects themselves. Keaton's ability to use the same object in manifold ways in the same frame of action is astonishing. Take, for instance, his use of the cannon (found in both *The Navigator* and *The General*).

Keaton plays (1) on the intrinsic qualities in each particular cannon and (2) on a new and uncommon use of the cannon itself. In the first case, there is usually something absurd, grotesque and preposterous about the cannon to start with. In *The Navigator* it is no larger than a toy and is pulled around by an endless string in which one can and does get one's feet hopelessly entangled; in *The General* it is enormous and has a curious way of swinging around on its axis, causing occasionally embarrassing surprises. When the cannon itself does not present a curious appearance, new and uncommon use is made of its properties as a weapon. In *The General*, using a steady-fire cannon, Keaton discovers an interesting vertical firing system (the consequences of which are unexpected but surprisingly fruitful) when, by pulling on the firing cord he causes the weapon to rotate on its axis and come to rest in a perilous but graceful equilibrium.

*　　*　　*

Keaton takes advantage of every situation. He never shirks an issue or, if he does, it's because he has already gleaned everything possible from the situation.

When he finds himself with the anarchist's bomb in *Cops*, he doesn't panic; he lights his cigarette with it. Only when he has accomplished this action does he fling the bomb away (like a dead match) and let what will happen happen.

This diverting of an object from its course already paves the way for the famous Keaton "turnabout", the origins of which we shall study later. The bomb thrown by the anarchist falls on the seat next to Keaton who fails to see it: gag. At the same time, things seem to be going badly for our hero. Second gag: Keaton lights his cigarette. The situation turns in our hero's favour. Third stage: another turnabout of the situation: the bomb explosion will cause Keaton the gravest difficulties. In this case, of course, a foreign element has intervened; this is not yet the form that Keaton's openness to the world and his way of approaching and using objects will take.

In *Paleface* Keaton is bound to a stake; after a short dance, the Indians decide to burn him. They go looking for wood, leaving one of their number behind to build the pyre around his feet. Meanwhile, Keaton has managed to unearth the stake. But instead of merely fleeing, as anyone else would do, he takes advantage of a moment when the Indian's back is turned and, when the Indian is off-screen, he moves the stake to another spot.[19] When the Indian returns, arms laden with an ovenful (the word applies here) of dead branches, he sees that Keaton is gone. The Indian, astonished, now perceives Keaton in the new spot. And while he goes to get the wood from the old pyre to start building a new one around Keaton, the latter, behind his back (the Indian remains on screen all the while this time) returns to the original spot. It is only after he has revealed his utter mastery of the situation that Keaton puts an end to it by

---

* In the burlesque cinema, which is a cinema of the immediate, of the here and now, if André Bazin's hidden-screen theory applies to the spectator (the adult spectator; the child believes unquestioningly that a character not seen is not there) it does not apply to the film characters themselves. As soon as a character is off-screen, he practically ceases to exist for the comic hero.

This was at least true for the primitive burlesque cinema; it rapidly disappeared. In his long films, as his style became ever more realistic, Keaton almost never used this kind of process.

knocking the Indian out with the stake.

If, incidentally, Keaton flees in *Paleface*, this is not because he is avoiding an unpleasant situation. He has every intention of returning and throwing himself into the thick of things, but when he does return, this time fortified with new elements, he'll bring new comic possibilities to the situation. After having milked every possible laugh from the chase and used spatial lines splendidly, Keaton comes crashing down, as we have already mentioned, on the Indian chief's paunch. This time he does not avoid the pyre, but this time he has taken the precaution to dress himself in asbestos; he turns the situation to his advantage; by mastering the fire, thanks to his ingenuity, he becomes a god.

* * *

The Paleface can serve as an excellent example to show how Keaton multiplies an object's functions to produce a gag.

The fire has burnt Keaton's bonds away. And now, as the smoke rises, enveloping him, and the flames begin to flag, totally unharmed but for an inevitably besooted face, Keaton takes out a cigarette, lights it, and begins to smoke. That is the first cigarette gag; in it Keaton affirms his perfect domination of the situation and shows his higher level of adjustment in terms of intelligence, quality, subtlety, physical resistance and supremacy.

He takes several steps towards the awe-inspired Indians, takes several puffs on his cigarette, and passes it to the Indian chief, who takes some puffs in turn, thereby sealing their friendship. And this is the second cigarette gag, the conversion of the cigarette into a peace pipe by the association of functions.

* * *

A variation on the chain of gags coming from one particular object is the *cascade of gags*.

In *Cops* Keaton sees a price card reading $5.00 leaning up against a horse and cart. In need of this means of locomotion, he pays five dollars to a man sitting on the pavement beside it, and drives away with his new aquisition. Actually, the price card really applied to a waistcoat on display. The man, who was not the owner of the horse and cart and who now finds himself with $5.00 in his hands, buys the waistcoat[20].

In the same film, two objects lead to a cascade of gags which are resolved into a single combination that brings forth another gag. The towel-rail which unfolds when he tries to attach it to the back of his car-load and the boxing glove he wears to protect his hand from dog-bites, will combine into an extraordinary directional indicator[21]. This open series gives one a foretaste of the concentrated form of Keaton's way of adjusting to the world.

But if these gags are remarkable and even smack of genius, there is nothing really extraordinary about the gags themselves[22]. If Keaton goes beyond the elementary level of the gag,[23] and if he develops the gag with an infinite complexity, what is really extraordinary is the way the gags succeed one another and his way of juxtaposing them.

Most of these gags have one thing in common: i.e. their results

[20] Let no one take the above for an illustration, based on a misplaced price-card, of the famous economics experiment that is the basis of buying on credit. (A person has left a sum of money with another person who uses the money to pay a whole series of debts, at the end of which the money returns to its starting point. The original person then returns to take back the money he has deposited. Everyone has been paid back although no money has been spent, since the same money used to pay everybody ends up back in its rightful owner's pocket).

[21] We have already seen what this directional indicator will do.

[22] In their structure, that is, and not by the attitude manifested towards them (although that seems to amount to the same thing) — and in respect to other existing gags.

[23] As defined by F. Mars: a situation, a particular action within this situation and a completion of this action "which is . . . both logical and preposterous" (Cf. p. 100 of the present work and no. 113, Nov. 60 of *Cahiers du Cinéma*, p. 25 article by François Mars, "L'Autopsie du Gag"). This is, in effect, the first form of the burlesque gag.

118

will either act favourably or unfavourably for Keaton.

We have seen that he never fails to take advantage of any situation or object that is offered. The greater the possibility for gags, the funnier the object or situation; at the same time, the possibilities will be all the more varied if they can be made to focus around one point in a contradictory fashion (the point in question being Keaton). In other words, an object or situation will have the greatest number of comic possibilities if it orients itself with regard to our hero both positively and negatively (in terms of success and failure) *at the same time*. The intensity of the possibilities matters more than the number. The gag will present the greatest variety of possibilities within the most concentrated form.

It is hardly astonishing, then, that Keaton should have introduced the *double turnabout* within the gag.

In *One Week* Keaton is towing his house to a new site. The house gets stuck on a railway crossing while he, momentarily oblivious to this, continues on his way. And now, from the right of the screen, comes a speeding train. We are given the scene in a wide shot from afar (the better to feel Keaton's impotence). But the train goes behind the house and leaves it undamaged. Surprise and joy. The house was not stuck on that track at all, but in front of it. But before we have even had time to admire the subtlety of this, and the clever positioning, another train comes roaring from the left, smashing the house to smithereens. There we have a complete turnabout of the situation[24].

Another example of this turnabout (in his favour, this time): in

[24] When we say that Keaton introduces the turnabout, we mean he carries what already exists in the normal gag further still. In as much as the gag will work either negatively or positively for Keaton, it involves a double turnabout, the turning from the positive (or the indifferent) to the negative, and, inversely, the turning from the negative to the positive.

A gag is always, to a certain degree, a turnabout: a simple fumble constitutes a turnabout in itself.

College Keaton has been chosen to be coxswain of the college sculling team by the team director but against the wishes of the team itself, the members of which consider him intellectual and incapable[25]. His rival decides to eliminate him. In the dressing room, before the race, he puts a sleeping powder in Keaton's tea. But Keaton, having clumsily dropped something into his cup, surreptitiously exchanges it for his rival's.

Keaton realises that he's not wanted on the team and, sad but conciliating, decides not to participate in the race. But meanwhile the insidious sleeping powder is taking effect on his rival. Keaton's team-mates, finding themselves without a coxswain, are obliged to call on him.

The events thus happen in three stages for Keaton. First he is the coxswain; then he's no longer the coxswain; and last he's the coxswain again (with, this time, his team-mates imploring him). Just as before, we have here a turnabout of the situation.

These turnabouts, be they positive or negative, owe nothing to Keaton.

In *One Week*, Keaton was taken off his guard (indeed it was the first and only time that a train got the best of him. He would later go on to prove he knew exactly how to deal with trains). The turnabout came from the intervention of a purely foreign element which though perhaps foreseeable, was ineluctable. In the last analysis, the turnabout only accomplished a momentarily retarded inevitability[26].

---

[25] Which is precisely why the director (the ineffable Snitz Edwards, his majordomo in *Battling Butler*) designated him for the job.

[26] One must not accord too much importance to this particular "failure"; had Keaton been in command of the train, things would have turned out differently. In any event, no one could have done better.

For all that, one could, by stretching things, turn this failure into a success. Who, better than Keaton, knows how to smash houses? And perhaps the house's ultimate destination was to come to this perilous rest on the railway tracks. But enough of vain conjecture ...

Pure luck is responsible for the turnabout in *College*[27].

A greater use of turnabouts due to outside intervention is in *Electric House*. The well-ordered house falls into disorder. The second abortive turnabout which takes place in the second part of the film does not really resolve the situation. Keaton more or less gets the house back under control — but only just.

And the final turnabout whereby Keaton escapes drowning because the pool empties miraculously — the ultimate effect of which is to fling him back into nature — is neither a victory nor a defeat for him, but rather a momentary reprieve.

Electric House, which concludes with things at a status quo, is a sort of rough draft of the Keaton turnabout as it would be perfected in his major films (we shall come to this later)[28].

The gag only reaches perfection in the double turnabout form when no outside element intervenes, when it results from the internal dynamism of the situation or object that Keaton must deal with, and as he deals with it.

This gag's perfection is manifest when it "crowns" a variation on an object. Let us take, for example, the chariot race in *The Three Ages*.

Keaton shows up for the race with his chariot transformed into a sled (first variation: re-conversion). During the race, one of the dogs harnessed to his chariot-sled, wounded, "gets a flat". Keaton unharnesses the dog and, taking out a second dog which had been hidden in the "boot" of his chariot-sled, changes dogs, putting the

---

[27] One could of course say that this pseudo-coincidence — Keaton's exchanging his cup for that of his rival — is a mark of Keaton's subtlety, and that this gag, far from reposing on a simple chance turnabout, is rather a "dialectical" gag based on Keaton's adjustment on a higher level; especially if one remembers how his team-mates, who snubbed him at first, now come after him.

[28] Although one might (once again) think that so ingenious a means of escaping death (a capricious pool) could be considered a positive adjustment to events.

wounded one in the place of the "spare" (second variation: assimilation dog-wheel and anachronism of spare tyre). The progression remains in Keaton's favour as he takes up the lead in the race.

Now a new gag begins: Keaton's rival throws a cat into the arena. *First turnabout:* the dogs start chasing the cat which, terrified, flees the track, followed by Keaton's dogs. *Second turnabout:* the cat, having gone once around the arena with Keaton's dogs on its heels, crosses the winning line and leads Keaton to victory.

In this instance the internal dynamics of the situation are responsible for the turnabouts. The dogs chase that cat and frighten it; the frightened cat runs at a dizzying speed; the dogs quicken their pace to catch the cat, and by so doing, despite the fact that they have gone far out of their way and Keaton's, bring him victory.

The result of this double turnabout is not a return to the point of departure but a going beyond it. For indeed, Keaton goes on to victory with so much more dash, elegance, virtuosity and superior mastery than he would ever have had without it; and this dizzying and turbulent trajectory — so familiar and wonderful a part of Keaton's films — which so masterfully places him and all his movements in space, is the concrete achievement of Keaton's form of higher adjustment, which belongs to him alone.[29]

The same crowning triumph is his in *The General*. In pursuit of the Northerners, Keaton prepares to use against them the curious bombarder-mortar-cannon he has had the foresight to hitch on to the back of his train. He loads the weapon with elegant pinches of cannon powder *(first variation:* cannon charge assimilated into salt-cellar). Keaton lights the weapon's fuse. The cannon fodder pops

---

[29] This has nothing in common with any ordinary victory.

out and, after describing a most graceful curve, drops a few feet away *(second variation:* simple turnabout, Keaton's fiasco. The cannon belches its projectile in a niggardly fashion).

But Keaton isn't one to let himself be bested. This time he stuffs the cannon full to the brim. Now we'll see what we'll see. He lights the fuse and, while it burns, returns to his driver's seat.

But on his way back to the tender he unfortunately uncouples the mortar truck, detaching it from the rest of the train. The liberated connecting hook drags along the track, jerking the weapon and causing the cannon to lower dangerously, until it's aiming directly at Keaton who tries to save himself. But in his panic he's ensnared his foot in the hook of the tender, and remains a captive directly in the cannon's line of fire. In a fit of panic he impotently throws a piece of wood at the cannon (a supreme detail this, adding to the gag's perfection). This solution proving ineffective, he faces the cannon, helpless.

It is now that Keaton the director, compensating for his energy, makes the track curve. The positions are thus the following: Keaton's locomotive takes the curve and is no longer in the cannon's line of fire; the Northerners' locomotive, on the other end of the curve, is. And just before the cannon itself takes the curve, the shot goes off!

Things happen in this double-trigger[30] gag in the following manner:

First stage: Determined to succeed, Keaton loads the cannon to the brim, to make it as effective as possible.

Second stage: Turnabout of events. The cannon he has taken such effort to load and make murderous, turns on him.

Third stage: New turnabout: the cannon shoots at its original target but now in a different and, to be sure, incomparable manner.

[30] We must say this now or never.

123

The developmental internal coherence: the same pigheaded obstinacy on the part of the cannon which led it to threaten Keaton turns the situation about so that it now fires on the Northerners.

Note that at the end of this double turnabout there is no pure and simple return to the original state of affairs. The aims of both Keaton and the cannon are achieved in an apotheosis of ordered intelligence, geometry and choreography. Both Keaton and the cannon surpass themselves, the former by his magnified action, the latter, its function enriched, by its added inventiveness and precision; Keaton makes the cannon do things it could never have done otherwise.

By his action Keaton enriches reality and gives it a new and unsuspected dimension; by enriching reality his own adjustment to it is on a higher level, the result of which is a supreme self-accomplishment[31].

The diagram of this gag, like that of the abovementioned gag from *The Three Ages*, is as follows:

(1) The affirmation of an intention by Keaton.

(2) The *negation* of Keaton's project by events.

(3) The *negation of the negation*. Keaton accomplishes his project and puts forth all his action, but on a higher level.

This gag form is evidence of a perfectly "dialectical" form of adjustment on Keaton's part[32] in the course of which the synthesis resolves the contradiction, through Keaton's masterful success

---

[31] It is of course understood that Keaton's actions cannot be judged according to usual norms and considered with traditional results in mind. If they could be, one might challenge Keaton's responsibility in the final turnabouts of the situation. The form counts more than the result itself. Keaton is only Keaton inasmuch as his form of adjustment is truly unique and different; and the way things happen is evidence of his remarkable mastery of spatial lines and the placing of things. This felicitous and wonderful combination of circumstances can only happen *in his presence*. It is thus clear that what happens does happen thanks to him even if, according to the usual criteria, he would not seem to be directly responsible for it.

Here Keaton the hero becomes confused with Keaton the director.

[32] If we may use the word.

THE GENERAL.

COLLEGE.

and an enrichment of reality. The gag structure is not circular but dialectical and incarnates Keaton's superior mode of adjustment to the world.

Note here that the solution is once again a question of the placing of elements in space.

This "dialectical" gag structure is a constant in Keaton's films; it can be found throughout. Examples are multiple and varied. But since we've started with *The General*, let's stay with *The General* which is a veritable treasure trove.

The Northerners have left a large log on the tracks. Just managing to stop his machine in time, Keaton scrambles down and lifts the log. But the locomotive, insufficiently braked, starts up, unbeknown to Keaton who has his back to it, his legs spread wide to give him a firmer stance. The moving engine's footplate slowly comes between his legs and lifts him, and so he finds himself astride the footplate of the ever-accelerating train, with the enormous log in his arms.

And now he espies a second log lying across the track. With an ease that is nothing short of stupefying, he hurls the log he is carrying in such a way that one of its ends strikes one of the ends of the obstructing log, thereby knocking it off the track.

Killing two obstacles with one throw, Keaton clears the tracks and can, once back in his driver's seat, take up the chase again. It was his original desire to go fast, very fast, that had turned against him in terms of the situation. But had it really? After all, his apparently reckless haste had enabled him not merely to become a masthead for his locomotive and, with the log in his arms, to take one of the most beautiful poses the cinema has ever seen, but also, thanks to his tense energy, will, ingenuity and precision, to clear the track of an obstacle without even slowing down his speed. What may have seemed like reckless haste was really nothing but an extraordinary ability to overcome obstacles after having even multiplied their resistance and malignity.

Other examples of double turnabout gags in *The General* (I lack space, alas, for longer descriptions): the gag in which, commanding an improvised battery, Keaton manages to use his recalcitrant sabre in a most unusual manner; the gag in which, thanks to an original (and subtle) vertical firing system, he annihilates an entire Northern company, although it was to be feared at one point that he himself would be the cannon's target; or the locomotive gag described earlier in which, by barely avoiding what would have been a fatal crash, he escapes once and for all from the Northerners in one of the most beautiful railway ballets that the screen or any other medium has ever known. In this gag his wonderful geometrical ingenuity is brought to a choreographical apotheosis.

Pursued by policemen in *Cops*, Keaton climbs a ladder leaning against a fence and, to keep his pursuers from climbing after him, rocks the ladder at the top so that, with a see-saw movement, it sets him down on the other side, in a courtyard.

But the see-saw possibilities of the ladder turn against him. Just before he can touch earth, one of his pursuers grabs the rising end of the ladder and holds on, restoring the equilibrium and maintaining the ladder in a horizontal position. The ladder indeed becames a see-saw with the fence top for an axis. Soon several cops enter the courtyard and grab hold of the other end. Keaton takes refuge in the centre, as the two groups of cops, each pulling on their side, keep the ladder horizontal.

At this moment Keaton perceives an imposing group of cops running to the aid of those on the street side. Seeing this, he runs to the courtyard side of the ladder and squats, holding on. Since the ladder's see-saw possibilities have turned against him, he will use it as a catapult. And sure enough, the pull of the "street" cops is too much for the "courtyard" cops who give over, and Keaton, in a graceful flying position, is propelled into space far out of their reach.

Thus Keaton, having revealed a ladder's see-saw qualities, finds the means to metamorphose the ladder into a catapult when those qualities turn against him. And the final turnabout proves once again his higher powers of adjustment; using an object he triumphantly enriches it, and that makes his triumph all the greater.

At the end of *Cops*, with every cop in the city after him, Keaton dives through an open doorway. Before he can close it, all the cops have pushed their way in, blocking the entrance with their black bulk. What's more, it turns out that the door was the door to the Central Police Station. The door closes. And opens a moment later to let out a thin black form, which locks it shut and throws the keys into a dust-bin. The thin black form is Keaton, of course.

Here the positioning is almost totally responsible for the turnabout and Keaton's self-surpassing; the positioning operates on the relations of masses. Take Keaton's well-defined and concentrated form, and try to drown it in a rough and formless mass, and you will always see the little black mass float to the top, calmly insolent, frail but sure of itself[33].

In *The Navigator* Keaton wants to make use of a curious little cannon to defend his boat from the natives. He comes on deck pulling it behind him on a long string, like a toy. He loads it carefully and lights the fuse. But while stepping backwards he catches his

---

[33] That the situation turns about one final time at the end changes nothing. The police chief's daughter has meanwhile intervened. And if Keaton "gives himself up", he does so voluntarily. His is pure and simple suicide. This is one of the rare times that Keaton is "unlucky in love" as one says. All of which goes to show that in a police chief's daughter the desire for order takes precedence over the desire for the higher and supreme values incarnate in Buster Keaton.

foot in the string and the cannon attached to it follows him. Keaton desperately tries to free himself from this cumbersome and dangerous toy. The natives rise up behind him just as the shot goes off; Keaton, stooping, avoids the projectile which terrifies the natives, and they flee.

Once again it is all a question of positioning here. It is because every element is in its proper place at the proper moment that events turn definitively in Keaton's favour. The little cannon, seemingly inoffensive but in fact a threat to Keaton (precisely because it seemed so inoffensive) turns out to be wonderfully effective.

In *College*, hired as a part-time barman, Keaton wants to imitate the professional dexterity of the ace barman he has just seen throw an egg in a glass. He tries this, but misses the glass. He tries a second egg, but misses again. But the second egg, missing the second glass, falls into the first glass which he missed with the first egg. Keaton takes this glass and serves his customer without any hesitation, but rather with a wonderful assurance, as if the whole thing had been planned.

And so another apparent bit of clumsiness is resolved on a higher level and, surpassing imitation, permits him to invent new forms.

The final gag in *Battling Butler*, described earlier, also takes on this turnabout-surpassing form. Keaton, now a great champion in his girl-friend's eyes, is in danger of becoming less than nothing should the real Battling Butler have his will with him. But by strengthening his own will, overcoming human limits with his energy, Keaton turns the situation to his advantage — and brings up from his own depths the means to do so. If Keaton's self-accomplishment is evident, it is the way Keaton surpasses himself that enriches the situation; who'd have thought that so much energy existed in the world, that one could so transcend oneself, that so hopeless a situation could turn out so positively? Keaton enriches the situation by an intensity of transcendence inconceivable without him.

To conclude in beauty (and since we are used to concluding with it) let us cite once more the final gag from *The General*, with Keaton able to kiss his girl at leisure at last, thanks to his heroism, and in a position (for the same reason) to salute the passing soldiers. By kissing his girl and saluting the soldiers *at the same time*, Keaton resolves and surpasses the contradiction in the circumstances. And this synthesis, which is his ability to do both things at the same time, is the mark of his success within a metamorphosed and enriched situation.

But this "dialectical" gag structure can stretch out and cover a sequence or even, if need be, an entire film.

The famous "domestication scene" of the kitchen and the ship itself in *The Navigator* takes this form, but there is a sort of cut in time. We are given successively a series of first phases: Keaton's unfortunate attempts; and then, later, a series of second phases: his success and self-surpassing.

The gag here which translates Keaton's superior mode of adjusting to events is, in its "dialectical" form, on the level of the sequence and almost of the entire film.

In *College*, too, (as we have already seen) this structure encompasses the quasi-totality of the film between the two phases of one huge "dialectical" gag.

Keaton, in a first part which represents the first phase of the overall gag, fails at every sport he tries.

In a second part, at the end of the film, taking up the situation at the point where he'd left it, Keaton adjusts magnificently and succeeds brilliantly (especially in the life-saving episode) in all he had originally failed at. And in so doing he transforms games of sport into games of love; to the sprint, the hurdle-race, the high-jump etc. he gives a wealth of love that these things would never have had but for him.

If need be, this form can be found in the general structure of all of Keaton's films, in this constructional symmetry we have already noticed in his scenarios.

And thus it seems that Keaton, by drawing from a coherent whole the contradictory possibilities of an object of situation as it applies to himself,[34] is led to a unique gag form which has a "dialectical" structure. The final gag attains a rare perfection, for it offers the greatest variety, the greatest inventiveness and the greatest concentration with a maximum of intensity.

This gag form, with its double turnabout aspect, defines Keaton's mode of adjusting to the world as "dialectic".

— In the first stage Keaton manifests a certain affirmation of himself with respect to a project centring either on a situation or an object.

— At the end of the first turnabout (negation) events resist Keaton, acting in an original and contrary manner towards him, creating unforeseen difficulties.

— But at the end of the second turnabout (negation of the negation) Keaton sets the situation straight by synthesising the contradictions through his surpassing himself on a higher plane.

This structure is thus evidence of Keaton's triumph and his supreme adjustment to the world in which he transcends himself on a higher plane, thereby engendering an enrichment of reality which itself contributes to his great success.

This elementary form of Keaton's action in the world, this fundamental attitude towards reality, can be summarised in the follow-

[34] Both favourably and unfavourably.

ing manner:

Keaton's openness to experience leads him towards things and brings him to accept everything that offers, be it totally unexpected and contradictory; when his openness works in his disfavour he manages, by surpassing himself, to impose himself on things in a new and different way; and his openness to experience, his calm affirmation of himself, become concrete on another plane, in a supreme self-accomplishment and enrichment of reality.

But one would have every right to say: What gives these turn-abouts meaning? Couldn't this series of upsets also end to Keaton's disadvantage and not to his advantage? Couldn't the turnabouts take on another order of succession rather than this "dialectical" order?

(1) Note first that the "dialectical" use of objects is Keaton's way of adjusting to the world as well as his way of controlling the world, for, by taking all of an object's possibilities into account (both for failure and success), this form succeeds, beyond all others, beyond all ideas of failure and success as ordinarily understood, in reconciling all of a situation's or an object's virtualities, and in giving them a perfect form of expression. All of which is a victory for Keaton — if only in his ability to re-invent things.

What's more, we need not look to the usual criteria on the "right and proper" use of an object to judge Keaton's ultimate success or failure, since his behaviour is constantly "different". And since his behaviour manages to show every possibility of a situation or an object, it is obligatorily successful.

(2) But most of all, note that in the examples cited, no gag solution is the product of chance; Keaton alone is responsible for every outcome, thanks to those qualities which we have never stopped insisting on: concentration, tenacity, bodily poise, athletic prowess,

wondrous energy, ingenuity, subtlety, resourcefulness, adroitness, intelligent placing, extraordinary sense of positioning, geometrical mastery of space, perfect visual harmony and choreographic beauty.

Let us be clear; we have no intention of making a god or "superman" a sort of "victory machine" of Keaton; he is not infallible. We have never meant to imply that he is the absolute master of all, and particularly of the universe. It is his form that matters when he deals with the world, and if he and his form triumph *most of the time* (not always and not systematically) that is because he never gives in and never gives up.

(3) The turnabouts could of course work to Keaton's detriment, but when there's danger of that, a foreign element intervenes. The situation is no longer the same. A new adjustment cycle begins for Keaton.

Seldom, "when he has had it out with them", do objects or situations play nasty tricks on Keaton.

(4) What helps convince us that Keaton's supreme form of adjustment to the world involves a "dialectical" use of objects, is that the general pattern of almost all his films tends to be, if fundentical, at least analogous[35]; which is to say that the successive trials he must undergo are usually resolved positively for him.

Most of Keaton's films are built along the following lines: Keaton is determined to accomplish something — usually for a woman: either he must "win" her by being glorious, he must overcome her father's resistance, or he must save her from various dangers. At the start things go badly for him, but at the end, "in a final sprint of gags"[36] he turns the tide *(Neighbours, The Playhouse,*

[35] There is not the same rigour in all of them, of course.

[36] Michel Mardore, review of *The Three Ages, Cahiers du Cinéma* no. 130, April 1962, p. 44.

My Wife's Relations[37], *The Three Ages, Our Hospitality, The Navigator, Sherlock Junior, The General, Seven Chances, Battling Butler, College, Steamboat Bill Junior, The Cameraman).*

Note that if Keaton's qualities are responsible for bringing gags to successful conclusions, the gags themselves are not conceived to bring out these qualities; on the contrary, Keaton's qualities appear as such precisely because Keaton can bring the gags to successful conclusions. But make no mistake: Keaton's qualities, personality and moral force are nothing other than his actions.

Note, too, that in most of the cases cited the successful conclusion is due to perfect positioning, thus perfect directing; all of which proves once again that Keaton's directorial genius stems from his ability to position himself and his action.

The point is not that this "dialectical" gag form is the only kind of gag form Keaton uses, but that it is the most perfect form, gathering as it does all the different aspects of his adjustment to the world, and showing them with the greatest comic intensity.

Nor ought one to reproach Keaton for not having used this form exclusively[38]. After all, he need not always start by failing; often and right from the start he succeeds, immediately presenting a supreme manner of adjustment.

Lastly, and most important: *by seeking to perfect the burlesque gag, Keaton discovers the driving form of his adjustment to the world,*

[37] Although it ends happily (whereas some of Keaton's films, especially the short ones, do not) there is in *My Wife's Relations* one of the rare examples of the double turnabout working to Keaton's detriment. But his situation from the beginning was not the most fortunate: not only is a repulsive shrew of a wife imposed on him, but her whole odious family as well. The first turnabout ends with everyone becoming mysteriously kind to him, after the discovery of a letter promising him an inheritance. But when the family discovers that the letter was not addressed to him at all (second turnabout) the untenable situation begins again. But have no fear, our hero escapes at the end. He leaves for Reno, thereby leaving his wife and her family forever (grounds for divorce: mental cruelty, no doubt.) This film is moreover remarkable for its von Stroheim level of atrociousness.

[38] And happily for that.

of his "world action" — nor is this because he wants to reveal "exemplary qualities", to give a certain meaning to his world action, or to deliver any message.[39]

The meaning of the gag structure only comes later; not Keaton's to worry about it. *Keaton's "world action" is not the fruit of ethical reflection but of comic practice.*[40] By merely trying to bring laughter, he creates new forms.

It is *our* duty to find the meaning of these forms; because they do have an objective meaning doesn't necessarily mean their creator was aware of it.

The use to which he puts the cinema-object may teach us something of the meaning of creation for Buster Keaton.

[39] This kind, for instance: "The world is man's. He must control it, no matter how hard it resists."

[40] Keaton's main goal perhaps was merely to make us laugh. But being a comic and cinematic genius, he spontaneously brought the gag to a rare degree of perfection.

6. Buster Keaton and the Cinema

IN *Sherlock Junior* and *The Cameraman*, Keaton incorporates the cinema itself into his gags. The two films, in fact, are about the cinema. These two are not the only films in which Keaton makes use of the cinema in one form or another. We have already seen how *The Three Ages* is a parody of *Intolerance;* and already in this film he uses the diplodocus as a crane — something between an oriental prince descending from his elephant and a crane operator. Keaton, regally perched atop the beast's long-necked little head, has the animal place him gently on the ground.

In *Free and Easy* Keaton plays a film director, but unfortunately I have not seen this particular film.

The cinema is thus a constant theme for Keaton. For that matter, the film milieu was a choice subject for almost all early cinema burlesque. But when treated by others (especially by Mack Sennett) it was treated precisely *as* a milieu; interest was focused on the behind-the-screen activities, the below-stage business of film-making and distributing. But the cinema as a filmable world and as a mode of expression was much more rarely looked into. Briefly, if there was much cinema in the cinema, there was little film in the film.

Keaton's originality lay in his use of the film within the film, and he used this not merely as the source of one gag but as the springboard of two films.

*   *   *

Keaton is a projectionist in *Sherlock Junior*. At one moment he "splits" in two and dreams he's an actor in the film he's projecting. At the start he fails to bring the imaginary world under control;

the transfer is not yet real; the screen canvas appears as such on the real screen. Keaton, with one foot in the imaginary world, still has the other in the real world, or, in other words, in the movie house.

Sitting down on a rock in this strange universe, Keaton finds himself (by scene changes in the projected film) on a reef surrounded by roaring waves; he would dive into the water to look at the shore, but the scene changes again and he dives into snow. Keaton has thrust himself unwanted into this new, strange universe, which acts in a new way on him, revealing, to quote Philippe Demun, "his radical otherness"[1].

Using a tracking shot, rare in Keaton's films,[2] he makes the dream screen devour the real screen. And now Keaton projects all his desires on to the dream screen[3], thereby becoming an extraordinary creature who succeeds at everything he tries. Extraordinary, yes, but hardly more so than the real Keaton who, we need scarcely add, is every bit as fantastic as the imaginary one. What makes the imaginary Keaton so fantastic is more that he is a projection of the real Keaton than a simple "dream creature".

A flying detective, he solves crimes, confounds criminals and wins the heart of his lady-love, snatching her from the villain's clutches. But just as he is about to triumph, Keaton drowns in "the river of dream compensation"[4].

He returns to reality. The mediocre gagman and scenarist, feeling they have done enough for the cause of cinema, go to the corner bar for a drink. But Keaton does not stop here. Though he failed to triumph

---

[1] Philippe Demun, "L'être et l'objet", *Contre-Champ*, no. 3, May 1962, p. 10.

[2] At this time the tracking shot was seldom used, although well known.

[3] If this film is psychologically rich, this is not because Keaton bothered much about psychology. One cannot help but admire his subtlety in this area; but this subtlety comes out in his gags, not in any free-for-all psychological mishmash.

[4] Ph. Demun, op. cit.

in his dream,[5] the dream has given him the impetus to straighten out his real-life difficulties, and he goes on to clear his name of the accusation of theft, to unmask the villains and to win back his love.

The turnabout here is not quite "dialectical". The cinema *qua* object acts towards Keaton representatively. If it is the occult cause for his turning the situation about, it is not the real cause. The cinema has set the example for Keaton, enabling him to turn the tide of events in the real world. If, however, one accepts the dream Keaton as the real projection of the real Keaton, one will realise that what Keaton did in the imaginary world was directly responsible for what Keaton goes on to do in the real world. He is the incarnation of his dream — by himself and for himself — the incarnation of his action, the prefiguration of the action he unconsciously decides to undertake in reality. The dream Keaton is nothing but the projection of the real abilities of Keaton (such as they appear elsewhere in all his films) which have not yet been affirmed.

Another turnabout follows this success. Framed in the window of the projection room (assimilation gag) Keaton imitates the gestures of the actors on the screen. He plays the greasy-haired lover. But suddenly the image changes and Keaton finds himself participating in a scene of "domestic bliss"; romantic love has changed into bourgeois comfort, and Keaton looks on, put out. This sudden change would seem to indicate that the cinema is turning against Keaton.

It is tempting to try to see in this film, in the way the cinema is used in it, a sort of parable about the act of creation. But what does one really see? Keaton, a cinematic creature, attempts to seize hold of what gives him life; he tries to penetrate the cinematic universe

---

[5] Which was nothing but a projection of his real situation; and perhaps he fails **precisely** *because* it was only a projection of his real problems.

and make use of it by a sort of alchemy of the image. Failure returns him to his human condition.

Certainly the door is open to this Faustian interpretation, and the temptation is great; and indeed Philippe Demun, with his extremely praiseworthy desire to accord this complex work its full importance, seems to have been carried away in his article in *Contre-Champ* — at least his words ran away with his thoughts when he wrote, in conclusion, quoting Rimbaud: "It seems that the efforts of the screen Keaton and the real Keaton coincide exactly. And that's where the word 'Faustian' takes on its full meaning. The poet, using magic, tries to eke out the secrets of life, to make himself master of its very essence. Keaton, a cinematic creature, tries to dominate the cinema. The loop is looped; struggling with the other, with the object, Keaton attacks his necessity, his life, that ultimate ontological object, the cinema. But the cinema refuses to let itself be tamed. The poet is the victim of that reality he wanted to master, whose toy, in reality, he is. 'Returned to the soil . . . and gnarled reality to hug . . . Peasant! . . .' And this strange parallelism between the creator and his image — man and his double each merging into the other — and the cry of despair in the face of a world that refuses to accept him, is perhaps what makes Keaton so near and dear to us, with his clear eye"[6].

This hypothesis, seductive though it may be, is nevertheless based on a rather confused idea of the role played by the cinema (as an imaginary world) in the turnabout of the situation within the film. And if, indeed, what emerges in this film is an (unpremeditated) reflection on the cinema, it need hardly be so desperate a one as all

---

[6] Philippe Demun, article cited, *Contre-Champ* no. 3, pp. 10-11. Demun elsewhere reveals a deeply penetrating insight into Keaton's work. What he says about *The Cameraman* makes up for his tendentious verbiage when talking about *Sherlock Junior* and leads one to believe that he must have become carried away with himself.

that.

For though the cinema can be considered the (occult) cause of the situation turnabout, it is only so insofar as the action prefigured in the dream (in the imaginary film within the film) is merely the projection of Keaton's real potential. The cinema is therefore only the "opportunity", the catalyst, for Keaton's self-surpassing; it is not the real cause. Besides which, though Keaton may be a poet, he is no "dreamer". He is a doer, a man of action.

The lesson (if lesson there be) is clear: the imaginary world reproduces the real world; it can only draw its substance from reality; if it compensates for reality, it nevertheless also returns one to reality. Keaton is thus perfectly aware of the representative aspect of the cinema, but he is not the dupe of its objective illusion and its magic possibilities.

Far from being a cry of despair, the end is rather like a pirouette in which Keaton summarises, in one sole gag, the general pattern of the film; and the end only reveals Keaton's genuine discomfort in the presence of the stultifying sweetness and bliss of bourgeois family life.[7]

The Cameraman enables us to see precisely how Keaton conceives of the cinema.[8] This is a continuation of *Sherlock Junior*, and in some way complements it.

With *The Cameraman* we are in the presence of a veritable "dialectical" use of the cinema-object. Keaton, a professional photo-

---

[7] There is moreover another turnabout which accentuates the "pirouette" aspect of the final gag, when Keaton has stood petrified before the vision of "domestic happiness". The last shot shows us Keaton with a real little family walking down a lane of rigorously aligned cottages, but taking us once again unawares (Keaton's ultimate use of fantasy, his great liberty), this vision does not *exactly* correspond to the one in the film within the film; for Keaton takes a stroll with a woman, yes . . . but he has exchanged the children for a litter of frisky pups.

[8] Let us stress the fact that if this conception exists in Keaton's work, he was not necessarily aware of it himself. He probably never bothered about finding himself an explicit definition of the cinema.

grapher, falls in love with a girl working for M-G-M. To win her heart he decides to become a newsreel photographer. He begins dismally, using the camera pathetically, failing with every reel he shoots. But later, thanks to a new use of the camera and the cinema, he triumphs.

Keaton's real self-surpassing here is due to a certain use of the camera which takes advantage of its dialectical possibilities.

The fundamental difference between *Sherlock Junior* and *The Cameraman* is that in the latter film he does not concentrate so much on camera-magic and illusions to be drawn from already-made films, but rather on films in the process of being made. And here we have him as a doer, not a contemplative dreamer.

When he first begins to use the camera, Keaton plays with its fantastic possibilities, with trick shots and illusory devices (his first try-outs show men in armour promenading down Fifth Avenue, divers diving up from the water to the diving-board, etc.). This conception of the cinema is reminiscent of *Sherlock Junior* and only shows a limited aspect of it.

In the second part of the film Keaton uses the camera merely to record reality.

In his realism Keaton may be defining an aesthetic; he is not defining any ontology of the cinematic image. Keaton is not the dupe of the literal realism of a certain kind of "live" cinema. At this early date he already shows *cinéma-vérité* up for what it is; when he does his "news-film" on the festival and fight in Chinatown, Keaton "fakes" reality to make it more truthful: when the combat, which has until now been a violent free-for-all, slows down, he starts it up again, returning a knife to an unarmed fighter about to abandon the fray, throwing bulbs which explode into the midst of the brawling crowd, etc.

142

COLLEGE.

COLLEGE.

144

COLLEGE.

STEAMBOAT BILL JUNIOR.

What Keaton offers us is not a direct copy of any immediate reality; already demonstrating his qualities as a director, he organises reality to make it more expressive, to make his image of it better correspond to truth; for the mere recording of an event by a camera does not automatically ensure the transference of the event's *real* reality into the film. To a certain extent, truth is the product of artifice. Keaton's "news-film" is more than a passive recording of reality; it is his personal way of seeing things; it is his "world action", the results of Keaton's actions with respect to events.

But if Keaton already reveals himself as a director in the Chinatown sequence, it is in the final news-film sequence that his directing takes the form of a genuine positioning of his "world action".

This newsreel, on which he'd filmed both the Chinatown ceremonies and the regatta, and on whose success depended his last chance to be accepted as a newsreel photographer for M-G-M, has been lost; to explain how it has been lost we must go back to the regatta itself.

During the regatta, in which Keaton's rival and girl-friend participate together, their boat capsizes. The rival shows himself for the cad he is by cowardly abandoning the unfortunate girl who is unable to break through the murderous circle that the outboard motor-boat, gone berserk, is describing around her. Keaton, witness to the event, heeds only the voice of his courage, drops his camera and goes to the aid of the drowning girl. Destroying the maddened boat by crashing into it with his own, he carries the girl back to shore and hurries off to the nearest chemist's for medicine and help. While he is gone the unconscious girl comes to her senses, and does so in the arms of the rival who, having swum to shore in the interim, claims to have saved her life and receives all the girl's sweet gratitude as a result.

Meanwhile Keaton's faithful companion, the little monkey, has filmed the whole scene; it is the little monkey who makes off with the camera and the film.

The newsreel is found, but Keaton, hopeless, certain he has failed in his task, leaves the M-G-M studios before it is shown. When it is shown, not only does it reveal Keaton's exceptional qualities as a newsreel photographer, but his heroic conduct as well. The head of M-G-M decides to hire him and the girl he loves at last recognises his merits.[9]

It therefore seems that, if Keaton records reality in a direct, simple style, without flourishes, what he records is not "Reality" but a certain manner of interpreting reality, which manifests itself in his "world action"; for, by exercising influence on the reality he is filming without clearly appearing to "direct" it, he ends up purely and simply by showing the way he himself acts in the world. And thus he demonstrates that directing is nothing but positioning with no apparent fancy touches[10] which preserves the credibility and the convincing aspect of things; and this positioning reveals — beyond its passivity and apparent indifference — a way of envisaging reality, since it is concretised in Keaton's very action in the world. Buster Keaton is Dziga Vertov and D.W. Griffith at the same time; he is Jean Rouch through the eyes of Luchino Visconti.

But we need not fear that Keaton's realism will make him lose his poetic qualities and make him "respectably middle-class".

It is not Keaton's final success, his "success in his work and his success in love" as traditionally understood, that matters here; what

[9] That the monkey and not Keaton filmed the incident changes nothing. This is merely one of those necessary artifices by which the "world action" is "positioned" in the *mise-en-scène*. When he made *The Cameraman* someone certainly had to be behind the camera while he was in front of it. Charlie Chaplin and Orson Welles have acted in almost all their films; neither have contested the fact that they were also the makers of these films.

[10] Simplicity nevertheless requires great art.

the girl realises is not so much that it was Keaton instead of the rival who saved her; rather, she becomes aware of Keaton's remarkable behaviour in the world, of his unassuming and sovereign heroism. The newsreel's realism confers on Keaton's form of adjustment a sort of undeniable and unchallengeable authenticity[11], which, far from hiding his physical, poetic and moral qualities, prepares the way for an all-the-greater self-accomplishment. If his "realistic" film ensures Keaton's higher adjustment to the world, it does not make Keaton into an anodyne being, for it is the faithful record of fantastic deeds; Keaton, by the simplicity of the positioning of his action, is revealed as an unchallengeably fantastic being.

And that is where his use of the cinema-object is really "dialectical". Keaton surpasses the possibilities of fantastic achievements linked to capacities for cinematic "faking" and so-called aggressive "direction" to bring them to a higher form — reconciling magic artifice and realism, representation and action — as reality gives birth to the fantastic side of action. And "that is why *The Cameraman*, this Newsreel by Buster Keaton of a newsreel by Buster Keaton, is probably his masterpiece."[12]

In Keaton's use of the cinema-object as a means of action on reality, there is both a surpassing of the contradictions of an object[13] and an enrichment of the object, which reveals all its potentials in a concrete manner at the same time as it permits Keaton's self-accomplishment.

The loop is looped; here again is that "dialectical" use of objects so characteristic of Keaton; and so *The Cameraman* quite simply

---

[11] Even if the image *is not* Keaton's action, but a reflection of it.

[12] P. Demun, "Une existence indéniable", review of *The Cameraman*, *Contre-Champ* no. 3, May 1962, p. 13.

[13] Contradictory aspects polarised either negatively or positively with respect to Keaton (failure or success).

leads us back to Keaton's attitude in his films, to his behaviour in the presence of events and things, to his "world action" and the linear simplicity of his positioning.

Note that Keaton does not use the cinema exclusively as an object having an end in itself[14]; for him it is a means of action and of world transformation.

By using the camera as a go-between, Keaton lays the foundation for his higher adjustment to the world, accomplishes himself and, by this accomplishment, transcends reality (as he does in *Battling Butler*).

The camera is an instrument, a means for him to surpass himself, precisely insofar as it is content to "position" the fabulous opera that is Keaton and his wondrous behaviour vis-à-vis things and events. Keaton's realism is thus linked to his "world action", i.e. to his action *in the* world, for remember that if we have defined Keaton's manner of viewing reality as a "world action" (in contrast to a "world vision" generally attributed to directors considered to be film-makers) this is precisely because his way of viewing the world is manifested uniquely in his activity in his films. And if he is fundamentally action, this tells us something already about the way the film-maker Keaton interprets the world; it attests to an action-conception of things and a will for transformation.

And *The Cameraman*, this monument of a film, is proof that by working at his craft of film-making and by giving himself completely to a cinema of enterprise, Buster Keaton surpasses and accomplishes himself; his cinema is not one of "romantic dreams" but rather one of realism, for it is a cinema in the process of being made which, making itself, seizes the real and transfigures it.

---

[14] An object that, moreover, he makes into a multiplicity of objects, revealing its infinite possibilities and integrating them.

What comes out of *Sherlock Junior* and *The Cameraman* is a certain conception of the cinema on Keaton's part; this conception can be defined as a realism established in Keaton's way of envisaging the world, i.e. above all as the terrain for an action.

Keaton places himself in turn on the level of "imaginary reality", on the level of representation — i.e. on the level of cinema-dream (based, as everyone knows, on an objective illusion of the cinematic image) — and then on the level of creation, of the cinema in the process of making itself. And, insofar as the cinema returns one to reality (not to a fixed passive reality but to a reality in movement) Keaton is led to make of the cinema a means of action on things, precisely insofar as the main purpose of directing is the simple and faithful positioning of an action.

And this, the creator's view of films and cinematic forms, brings us back to what we said on the conception of the *mise-en-scène* and the cinema in general which stands out in Keaton's work.

Is this to say that Keaton is an extra-lucid creator, and, consequently, a hyper-cerebral one? Are we in the presence of a sort of "Treatise on the Cinema and Cinema-Directing" by Buster Keaton? Is *The Cameraman* to Buster Keaton what, for example, *The Little Organon for the Theatre*[15], is to Bertolt Brecht i.e. an exposé of his conception of his art?

Of course not. The method with which *The Cameraman* seems to cross-check Keaton's conception of the cinema is certainly revelatory of his lucidity, but only insofar as it is the sign of the *coherence* of his work. This lucidity is not reflective lucidity, it is merely the way he exercises his cinematic art, it is in the service of the cinema, it is the lucidity of a man who is not paralysed by theories and who,

---

[15] An unfair comparison, perhaps; *The Little Organon for the Theatre* is not a play whereas *The Cameraman* is a film.

151

raising not theoretical problems, merely *does*, and by so doing gives a more precise idea of his art than any emitted by any of our self-styled definers of "essences" and "specifics"; this lucidity is what gave birth to some of the most coherent and beautiful films, not in the comic cinema alone, but in the world cinema from its beginnings to the present time.

The "reflection" on the cinema in *The Cameraman* is no reflection at all. It is merely the reflection of the way in which Keaton implicitly conceives of the cinematic art in his films. Nor is the way in which Keaton makes films — the way he projects a certain image — premeditated either.

Keaton probably never bothered to make his films from any particular angle, nor did he ever adopt any intransigent position on "realism". Once again, this must be stressed. He created *forms* and if these forms have any extraordinary coherence, Keaton's genius alone is responsible for that.

We repeat: Keaton's main desire was to make people laugh. By perfecting his pantomime and the burlesque gag, he developed the "form of adjustment to the world" that stands out in his films. Similarly, by practising the comic cinema, such as it was done during the silent era, and by making it a part of himself, he developed his style. The "world action" and style he expressed in his films are only reflections of his real possibilities — transposed to the level of the comic and cinematic creator — and the straight, direct way that he employed the cinema.

If the ethics which stand out in Keaton's films are those of action and transformation, that is because he proved *concretely*, while shooting his films, that he was capable of the impossible. And if Keaton considers the cinema to be a means of action on reality, and if his style consists above all in the simple positioning of his "world action", this is because his conception of the cinema as well as his style is but the reflection of this cinema in the process of making itself, of this burlesque cinema which took itself out into the street, this "Cinema of enterprise"[16] which was the comic cinema of the silent era, the inheritor of the Mack Sennett tradition.

Finally, by making concrete in his films a certain form of realism which conceives of the cinema[17] as a means of action on reality and conceives of directing as a positioning that is expressive (most credibly and most unchallengeably, financially speaking) of a certain way of envisaging things, Keaton defined an aesthetic which was a most important and modern contribution to the cinema.

Incontestable as that may be, one must not lose sight of the fact that Keaton only defines an *aesthetic* insofar as he defines an *ethic;* that he only defines an *ethic* insofar as he defines a *style* (i.e. forms); and that he only defines a *style* insofar as he defines a *practice.*

The aesthetic expressed in his films is the result of the active and transforming vision of things which is Keaton's "world action"; just as this is the result of the way Keaton puts forms together in his cinematic comic practice.

And so we have turned full cycle again. We can return, after this digression on Keaton's use of the cinema-object, to Keaton's practice as expressed in his dialectic use of objects.

---

[16] As A. Martin termed Keaton's cinema, op. cit., *Cahiers du Cinéma*, no. 86, p. 86.

[17] Going beyond, on the one hand, escape-cinema and, on the other, the "ontological" realism of the cinematic image.

7. Extensions of Keaton's Work

NOW that we have witnessed Keaton's higher form of adjustment, how vain seem the interpretations of those who only see in his work the manifestation of a radical strangeness or an impotence in the face of the world.[1] Having ascertained that not merely objects but whole huge mechanical entities as well (the cinema included) are Keaton's favourite territory for confronting the world, none will ever find in him that pseudo-obsession with the mechanised world we live in (incarnation of man's fear of life and the future) that has constantly been drummed into our ears. And those who speak of that obsession in Keaton are merely, like *Sherlock Junior*, projecting their own everyday fears onto the screen.[2]

Besides, why should anyone bestow this panicked terror of objects (mechanised or not) on a man whose favourite distraction was to make the utmost use of the infinite possibilities of such objects?

Here is what one observer writes:

"The front room [she is talking about Keaton's bungalow when Keaton was gagman at M-G-M] is entirely consecrated to the mechanical arts. Impressive mechanical constructions are erected on huge tables. Buster loves inventing gadgets. It's his greatest pride. He

---

[1] Of course, as we have already said, every comic hero is "strange" because he is funny.

[2] Which is to say that they live these ideas every day, and, especially, these ideas are those of their day-to-day life.

himself insisted on doing me the honours of his *great infernal nut-cracking machine*.

"The machine which stands on a table must be at least three feet high. It looks extremely complicated. This is how it works: a crane, put in motion, picks a choice nut from a gunny sack. The crane raises the nut to the top of a slide and drops it; the nut begins its slide, and after meandering from small a to big A, then from small b to big B, it drops into a basket. The basket conveys it from C in C' to a transporter bridge. From there, after a lot of comings and goings intended to soften it, the nut crosses several canals and inclined planes, and then, suddenly set on its vertical, comes to a raised platform on which it descends, progressively, until it arrives at last beneath a kind of steam-hammer in the form of a mallet which, at the proper moment, rises, comes down, and . . . misses.

"There's nothing for it but to begin all over again"[3].

Is there in this any insurmountable panic in the face of mechanised objects? Nonsense! Why make of this imperial, tranquil little man, another victim of our "Kafkaesque world"?[4]

---

[3] Henriette Nizan, "Portrait de Buster Keaton", *Le Magasin du Spectacle*, no. 4, August 1946.

Because the hammer misses the nut there is no reason to see here a symbol of Keaton's terror of mechanisation; rather let us laugh with the inventor, and admire his profound mastery.

Cf. also "All his gags are drawn from laws of space and time. By using pennies like people, he makes them walk like people, and act like actors in a play. A good comic scene is often the result of more mathematical calculations than a work on mechanics." (Buster Keaton, *Bifur*, no. cited).

And how would those gentlemen who so enjoy endowing Keaton with their own fears interpret the matter, if Keaton, inventing gags, used pieces of money whose movements he regulated in terms of their mechanical make-up (in the scientific, non-Bergsonian sense of the term)? That he has done so because comedy is nothing but the expression of man's horror of mechanical objects? Is comedy for Keaton nothing more than a kind of exorcism of this horror? An attempt to exorcise it?

Let's be serious. Let's stop looking in Keaton's films for what we want to find, and see them for what they are. Let's have done with that "pessimistic" conception that has it that "when one laughs, it's to keep from crying." Bergson isn't dead for nothing.

[4] For that matter, if this problem is ever studied seriously some day, it may turn out that Kafka himself wasn't quite so "Kafkaesque" as others make him. Already, some think that . . .

Others, who do recognise Keaton's remarkable adjustment capacities, have an occasional tendency to minimise them by declaring them to be solely his defence faculties against the universe.

When André Martin writes: "But I am always staggered by Keaton's natural, contagious and probably unconscious wisdom which reduces the representation of a hostile and sorrowful world, necessary to clowns, to a whole universe of fundamental adversity, of pure necessity; no more (for that opens the door to an eloquence which is suspect) but no less (with all that that awakens of essential feelings)"[5] we cannot help but agree with him insofar as he stresses Keaton's self-surpassing and his stubborn refusal to be defeated by things, rather than a sort of self-pity in defeat; but there is something in the words "fundamental adversity" and "pure necessity" that one queries, for they seem to imply that Keaton is up against a kind of immutable destiny, and that try as he might to resist it, he will eventually have to submit to it.

In the same token, when Martin writes: "With scornful anxiety, with an unexpressed but nagging anguish, Keaton voyages through space, not the space of inadvertence but the space of adversity and necessity. Obstinate but not tense, advancing beneath his little hat as flat as the blue line of the Vosges, he goes forward with a stoic serenity, and would never dream of fleeing"[6] — by insisting on the "scornful anxiety"[7] or on the "stoic serenity" with which Keaton goes forward, he seems to be bringing grist to the mill of those who

[5] Op. Cit., *Cahiers du Cinéma*, no. 86, August 1958, pp. 28-29.

[6] Ibid, p. 26.

[7] We would not dream of saying that Keaton's face *never* reveals "an unexpressed but nagging anguish" but, simply, such an attitude is not natural to him and his normal expression is one of intense concentration.

Of course it does sometimes happen that, when, for a *brief* instant, his energy abandons him and he gives way to panic before an object or situation, his grave and beautiful mask is congealed, more or less cataleptically, into an expression of "scornful anxiety" — but his moral force never abandons him for long, and he always ends by reacting in his own inimitable way.

only want to see in Keaton's abilities to bring order to the universe a manifestation of the instinct for survival.

*   *   *

At the other extreme, some have occasionally heralded Keaton as the guardian of the established order. In point of fact, his proven faculties for bringing order to the universe are never used to re-establish the status quo, but rather to establish a higher order. As we have seen, Keaton never merely re-establishes anything; he always goes beyond.

If, in the end, Keaton is as free as Chaplin and the Marx Brothers, his freedom is not to be confused with their anarchism. It is much more concrete. Insofar as he is never content merely to destroy the established order of things, but that he brings to them a higher order, Keaton's comedy is perhaps, *in its form* more complete than either Chaplin's or the Marx Brothers'.

Keaton's originality, of which he is probably unaware, lies in his having introduced the concept of self-surpassing within the comedy. His triumph is not the result of a shrinking into himself, or the mere preservation of his integrity or of withdrawing into a protective shell, but rather of an expansion of himself, of his openness to the world. It is because he welcomes the world with open arms[8] that he brings down troubles on his head which must be overcome, and obstacles in the way of things that must be faced.

The victory over the world which Keaton's kind of higher adjustment represents — that higher adjustment which helps him to resolve the contradictions of an object or situation (insofar as they affect him) while, at the same time, he accepts their multiple and

---

[8] Even if it takes the form of an attentive concentration which might pass as a desire to refuse to receive.

varied qualities — is marked by a real enrichment of the reality of things. Keaton's self-accomplishment is the result of an accomplishment of the world, just as the accomplishment of the world is the result of Keaton's self-surpassing. For Keaton, above and beyond his mere confrontation of things either positively or negatively, imposes a new dimension on them.

And thus we find Keaton in this multiform adjustment (ingenuity, energy, integration with space and things, beauty, excellence, self-accomplishment) with the same openness to events and things that motivated him at the start and which, as he confronted the resistance of the universe, pushed him to surpass himself and, by enriching reality, to adjust over again on another level, with the same openness to events and things that . . .

Once again the loop is looped, and Keaton, at the end of *The Cameraman*, after having achieved a marvellous metamorphosis of himself and of concrete reality, is once again wide open to the call of the world and ready to continue down that path on which man and life, engendering one the other, find their self-accomplishment one in the other, in a cycle that is not an eternal return but an eternal development.

Some may deplore Keaton's silence as to what must be done; they may regret that Keaton's films do not show us the world as it is in reality, that his scenarios only deal with a limited portion of reality, and a hardly revelatory one, that they lack those famous backgrounds which are the joys of Chaplin's films.

But there exist manners of being, *forms* of action which indirectly reveal a certain reality and teach us perhaps just as much about the world as great speeches do, no matter how great their beauty.

If Keaton is a poet because he gives an undreamed-of resonance to things, he does not do so within a compensating romantic poetry, but in the framework of that poetry which "must have practical truth for a goal", as Éluard turned Lautréamont's words; Keaton's poetry is a poetry of action. By practising this poetry on the world, the world is metamorphosed and transfigured in a real self-accomplishment of man. And if it is true that modern poetry was born one day, with Rimbaud, out of the will to "change life", Keaton is one of our most modern poets.

But Keaton did not expect us to read all this in his films; he offers no message; if his "world action" seems to imply so much, it is above all the action of a craftsman, of a great comedian, of a man of the cinema.

Similarly, if Keaton's contribution to the Seventh Art is considerable, this is not because he tried to be an "Artist", but because he strove to bring out cinematically, as simply and as effectively as possible, his comic attitude and his action in the world. A man can be a great artist without trying to be one.

Keaton's genius lies in his having engendered a work which is the expression of himself because it is undeniably coherent in its forms, and, consequently, in its implications; it is in that that one recognises a creator.

Buster Keaton's "world action" expresses itself visually in his bodily poise, his dynamic equilibrium, and in the perfect geometry of his being in space; it finds its successful aesthetic expression, using the burlesque gag, in the dialectical use of comic objects and situations; and interweaves the two forms to bring one to life through the other, since it is Keaton's perfect bodily mastery and perfect mastery of space that enables him to reach that higher adjustment at the end of a gag, just as it is the dialectical use of objects and situations that calls forth this perfect image and this beauty. And if this "world action" reveals the person's progress, there's nothing surprising in the fact that it brings laughter. No doubt, as Spinoza said, "joy" is "the passion which enables the mind to pass to a greater perfection."

And if Buster Keaton is one of the greatest creators in the history of the cinema, that's also not surprising because, as another philosopher said, "art is the greatest joy man can offer himself"[9].

---

[9] It was this philosopher (Karl Marx) that Keaton was reading as he scratched his left ear with his foot.
Please do not think, because of some things that have been said in this book, that we are trying to make of Keaton an adept of dialectical materialism.

suppressing in the fact that in things here and there. No doubt, as someone said, "Joy" is the passion which enables the mind to pass to a greater perfection."

And it might, Reason is not of the greatest creator in the history of the dream, that's also not surprising because, as another child—another said, "art is the greatest joy man can enjoy himself".

THE CAMERAMAN.

8. Provisional Conclusion

THIS essay is not a be-all and end-all. Much remains to be done. Another study is called for, that would examine the origins of Keaton's kind of comedy, and look for its significance in respect to that reality from which he issued. In other words, Keaton's comedy must be returned to its concrete origins, and, through a biographical, sociological and aesthetic study of the *man* Keaton, one might discover what the comedy Keaton incarnates is the real expression of.

It would be particularly interesting to develop in detail some things we have only sketched out, such as, to what degree Keaton's films were influenced by the climate of the "enterprise" cinema so important in the early days of the silent cinema.

It would also be interesting to ask oneself just how much the fact that he was born into a mechanised society in full development oriented Keaton towards this particular kind of comedy and the particular form of adjustment he manifests. For this one ought to look at American burlesque as a whole, not merely at Keaton. Lack of space and lack of time has made it impossible to do this. We hope that some day someone will undertake this enormous task, which will be a valuable aid in understanding American burlesque in general and Keaton's burlesque in particular.

QUI VOUS LAISSE SUR VOTRE FAIM
CAR BUSTER QUI TONNE
ETONNE ET LES TOMES
N'Y CHANGERONT RIEN.

Filmography

PARAMOUNT FAMOUS PLAYERS LASKY. *Producer:* Joseph Schenck.

COMIQUE FILM CORPORATION

Roscoe (Fatty) Arbuckle Comedies. 2 reelers.

Director of whole series: Fatty Arbuckle. *Players:* Fatty, B. Keaton, Al St. John.

1917

THE BUTCHER BOY with Josephine Stevens, Arthur Earle, Agnes Neilson. — **A RECKLESS ROMEO** with Corrine Parquet, Alice Lake. — **THE ROUGH HOUSE** — **HIS WEDDING NIGHT** with Josephine Stevens — **OH DOCTOR!** — **CONEY ISLAND** with Alice Lake, Stanley Pembroke.

1918

OUT WEST with Alice Lake, Joe Keaton. — **THE BELL BOY** with Alice Lake, Joe Keaton, Charles Dudley. — **MOONSHINE,** *Photography:* George Peters. *Players:* Alice Lake, Joe Bordeau. — **GOOD NIGHT NURSE.** *Photog.:* George Peters. *Player:* Alice Lake. — **THE COOK** with A. Lake. — **A COUNTRY HERO** with A. Lake.

1919

(without Al St. John but with Molly Malone):
BACK STAGE with Teddy (a dog). — **THE GARAGE** — **THE HAYSEED** with Teddy (a dog).

METRO PICTURES

1920

THE SAPHEAD (Full-length film) *Director:* Herbert Blake. *Prodduction Supervisor:* Winchell Smith. *Scenario:* June Mathis, adapted from the stage play, *THE HENRIETTA* by Bronson Howard. *Photography:* Harold Wenstrom. *Distributor:* Metro Pictures Corp. *Players:* B. Keaton, William H. Crane, Odette Tyler, Irving Cummings, Jeffrey Williams, Katherine Albert.

METRO PICTURES. Buster Keaton Comedies (2 reelers). *Producer:* Joseph Schenck.

ONE WEEK. *Scenario and direction:* Buster Keaton and Eddie Cline. *Players:* B. Keaton, Sybil Seely. — **CONVICT 13** (idem) — **THE SCARECROW.** *Scen. and Dir.:* B. Keaton and E. Cline. *Players:* B. Keaton, Sybil Seely, Al St. John — **NEIGHBOURS** *Scen. and Dir.:* B. Keaton and E. Cline. *Players:* Virginia Fox, Joe Roberts.

1921

THE HAUNTED HOUSE. *Scen. and Dir.:* B. Keaton and E. Cline. *Players:* B. Keaton, Virginia Fox, Joe Roberts, E. Cline — **HARD LUCK.** *Scen. and Dir.:* Idem. *Players:* Idem (less E. Cline) . — **THE HIGH SIGN.** *Scen. and Dir.:* Idem. *Player:* B. Keaton.

BUSTER KEATON PRODUCTIONS INC.

THE GOAT. *Scen. and Dir:.* B. Keaton and Malcolm (Mal) St. Clair. *Players:* B. Keaton, Virginia Fox, Mal St. Clair.

ASSOCIATED FIRST NATIONAL. *Producer:* Joseph Schenck.

THE PLAYHOUSE. *Scen. and Dir.:* B. Keaton and E. Cline. *Players:* B. Keaton, V. Fox. — **THE BOAT.** *Scen. and Dir.:* Idem. *Players:* B. Keaton, Sybil Seely — **THE PALEFACE.** *Scen. and Dir.:* B. Keaton and E. Cline. *Player:* B. Keaton.

1922

COPS. *Associate Producer:* Comique Film Corp. *Scen. and Dir.:* B. Keaton and E. Cline. *Players:* B. Keaton, V. Fox. — **THE ELECTRIC HOUSE.** *Assoc. Prod.:* B. Keaton Prod., Inc. *Scen. and Dir.:* B. Keaton and E. Cline. *Players:* B. Keaton, V. Fox, Pop (Joe) Keaton, Ma Keaton. — **MY WIFE'S RELATIONS.** *Assoc. Prod.:* B. Keaton Prod. Inc. and Comique Films Corp. *Scen. and Dir.:* B. Keaton and E. Cline. *Players:* B. Keaton, Kate Price, Monty Collins, Wheezer Doll. — **THE FROZEN NORTH.** *Assoc. Prod.:* Idem. *Scen. and Dir.:* Idem. *Players:* B. Keaton, Freeman Wood, Bonny Hill, Joe Roberts. — **THE BLACK-SMITH.** *Assoc. Prod.:* Comique Films Corp. *Scen. and Dir.:* B. Keaton and Mal St. Clair. *Players:* B. Keaton, V. Fox. — **DAYDREAMS.** *Assoc. Prod.:* B. Keaton Prod. Inc. *Scen. and Dir.:* B. Keaton and E. Cline. *Players:* B. Keaton, Renée Adorée.

1923

THE BALLOONATIC. *Assoc. Prod.:* Idem. *Scen. and Dir.:* Idem.

Players: B. Keaton, Phyllis Haver. — **THE LOVE NEST.** *Ass. Prod.:* Idem. *Scen. and Dir.:* Idem. *Player:* B. Keaton.

METRO PICTURES CORP. *Prod.:* Joseph M. Schenck. *(Full-length films).*

THE THREE AGES. *Dir.:* B. Keaton, *Scen.:* Jean C. Havez, Joseph A. Mitchell, Clyde Bruckman. *Photog.:* William McGann and Elgin Lessley. *Décors:* Fred Gabourie. *Players:* B. Keaton, Margaret Leahy, Wallace Beery, Joe Roberts, Lilian Lawrence, Horace Morgan, Oliver Hardy.

OUR HOSPITALITY. *Dir.:* B. Keaton and Jack Blystone. *Scen.:* Idem. *Photog.:* E. Lessley and Gordon Jennings. *Players:* B. Keaton, Natalie Talmadge, B. Keaton Jr., Joe Keaton, Kitty Bradbury, Joe Roberts.

1924

SHERLOCK JUNIOR. *Dir.:* B. Keaton. *Scen.:* Idem. *Photog.:* E. Lessley and Byron Houck. *Decors:* F. Gabourie. *Costumes:* Clare West. *Players:* B. Keaton, Kathryn McGuire, Joe Keaton, Jane Connelly, Ford West, John Patrick, Ward Crane.

THE NAVIGATOR. *Dir.:* B. Keaton and Donald Crisp. *Scen.:* Idem. *Photog.:* Idem. *Décors:* Idem. *Players:* B. Keaton, Kath. McGuire, Frederick Vroom, Noble Johnson, Clarence Burton, H. M. Clugston.

1925

SEVEN CHANCES. *Assoc. Prod.:* B. Keaton Prod. Inc. *Dir.:*

B. Keaton. *Scen.:* Idem, adapted from the play by Roy Cooper Megrue. *Photog.:* Idem. *Players:* B. Keaton, Roy Barnes, Snitz Edwards, Ruth Dwyer, Frankie Raymond, Jules Cowles, Erwin Connelly.

GO WEST. *Assoc. Prod.:* Idem. *Dir.:* B. Keaton. *Scen.:* Raymond Cannon, from an idea by B. Keaton. *Photog.:* E. Lessley and Bert Haines. *Players:* B. Keaton, Howard Truesdall, Kathleen Myers, Brown Myers.

1926

BATTLING BUTLER. *Dir.:* B. Keaton. *Scen.:* Paul Smith, Albert Boasberg, Charles Smith, Lex Neal, from the novel by Stanley Brightman and Austin Melford, adapted by Ballard McDonald. *Photog.:* J. Devereux Jennings and Bert Haines. *Players:* B. Keaton, Sally O'Neill, Snitz Edwards, Francis McDonald, Mary O'Brien, Tom Wilson, Eddie Borden, Walter James, Buddy Fine.

UNITED ARTISTS. *Producer:* Joseph M. Schenck.

THE GENERAL. *Dir.:* B. Keaton. *Original Idea:* B. Keaton and Clyde Bruckman, adapted by A. Boasberg and C. Smith. *Photog.:* Idem. *Technical Editor:* Fred Gabourie. *Editing:* Sherman Kell. *Players:* B. Keaton, Glenn Cavander, Jim Farley, Marian Mack, Frederick Vroom, Joe Keaton, C. Smith, Frank Barnes.

1927

COLLEGE. 6 reels. *Dir.:* James W. Horne. *Scen. and adaptation:* Carl Harbaugh and Bryan Foy. *Photog.:* Idem. *Montage:* Idem. *Players:* B. Keaton, Ann Cornwall, Flora Bramley, Harold

Goodwin, Buddy Mason, Grant Withers, Snitz Edwards, Florence Turner.

1928

STEAMBOAT BILL JUNIOR. 7 reels. *Dir.:* Charles F. Reisner. *Scen. and adapt.:* Carl Harbaugh. *Photog.:* Idem. *Edit.:* Idem. *Players:* B. Keaton, Ernest Torrence, Marion Byron, Tom Lewis, Tom McGuire.

THE CAMERAMAN. 8 reels. *Assoc. Prod.:* B. Keaton Prod. Inc. *Dir.:* Edward Sedgwick. *Scen.:* Clyde Bruckman and Lex Lipton. *Continuity:* Richard Schayer. *Photog.:* E. Lessley and Reggie Lanning. *Editing:* Hugh Wynn. *Players:* B. Keaton, Marceline Day, Harold Goodwin, Sidney Bracy, Harry Gribbon.

METRO-GOLDWYN-MAYER. *Prod.:* Joseph M. Schenck.

1929

SPITE MARRIAGE. 9 reels. *Dir.:* Ed Sedgwick. *Scen.:* L. Lipton. *Adapt.:* Ernest S. Pagano. *Cont.:* R. Schayer. *Photog.:* R. Lanning. *Edit.:* Frank Sullivan. *Players:* B. Keaton, Dorothy Sebastian, Edward Earle, Leila Hyams, Will Bechtel, John Byron, Hank Mann.

(Last film produced for Keaton by Joseph Schenck).

THE HOLLYWOOD REVUE. 13 reels. *Dir.:* C. F. Reisner. *Prod.:* Harry Rapf. *Dances and Show Pieces:* Sammy Lew. *Dialogue:* Al Boasberg and Robert E. Hopkins. *Décors:* Cedric Gibbons. *Orchestral arrangements:* Arthur Lange. *Lyrics:* Joe Goodwin. *Music:* Gus Edwards. *Photog.:* John Arnold and Irving G. Ries.

Costumes: David Cox. *Players:* The Stars of M-G-M incl. B. Keaton, Lionel Barrymore, Joan Crawford.

1930

FREE AND EASY. 10 reels. *Prod. and Dir.:* Ed. Sedgwick. *Idea:* R. Schayer, adapted by himself and Paul Dickey. *Dialogues:* Al Boasberg. *Music and Lyrics:* Ray Turk and Fred E. Ahlert. *Photog.:* Leonard Smith. *Décors:* Cedric Gibbons. *Editing:* William Le Vanway. *Players:* B. Keaton, Anita Page, Fred Niblo, Robert Montgomery, Lionel Barrymore, Trixie Friganza.

DOUGH BOYS. 9 reels. *Prod.:* B. Keaton Prod. Inc. *Dir.:* Ed Sedgwick. *Scen.:* R. Schayer, from an idea by Al Boasberg and Sidney Lazarus. *Photog.:* Idem. *Edit.:* Idem. *Players:* B. Keaton, Sally Eilers, Cliff Edwards, Edward Brophy, Victor Potel, Arnold Korff, Frank Mayo, Pitzy Katz.

1931

PARLOR, BEDROOM AND BATH. *Prod.:* B. Keaton. *Dir.:* Ed Sedgwick. *Scen.:* R. Schayer, from the play by Charles W. Bell and Mark Swan. *Dial.:* Robert E. Hopkins. *Photog.:* Idem. *Editing:* Idem. *Players:* B. Keaton, Charlotte Greenwood, Reginald Denny, Cliff Edwards, Dorothy Christy, Sally Eilers.

BUSTER SE MARIE (French version of above film). *Dir.:* Claude Autant-Lara, *Players:* B. Keaton, Françoise Rosay, Mona Goya, André Luguet, Jeanne Helbling, André Berley, Georges Davies, Rolla Norman, Charles Boyer.

SIDEWALKS OF NEW YORK. 8 reels. *Prod.:* B. Keaton Prod. Inc. *Dir.:* Jules White and Zion Myers. *Scen.:* George Landy and

Paul Gerald Smith. *Dial:*. R. E. Hopkins and Eric Hatch. *Photog.:* Idem. *Players:* B. Keaton, Anita Page, Cliff Edwards, Frank Rovan, Norman Philips, Jr., Sid Taylor, Frank Larue, Clark Marshall.

1932

SPEAK EASILY. *Dir.:* Ed Sedgwick. *Players:* B. Keaton, Thelma Todd, Jimmy Durante, Hedda Hopper.
THE PASSIONATE PLUMBER. 8 reels. *Prod.:* B. Keaton Prod. Inc. *Scen.:* Lawrence E. Johnson, from the play by Jacques Deval. *Dial.:* Ralph Spencer. *Photog.:* Norbert Brodine. *Mont.:* William S. Gray. *Players:* B. Keaton, Jimmy Durante, Irene Purcell, Polly Morgan, Gilbert Roland, Mona Maris. — **LE PLOMBIER AMOUREUX** (French version) *Dir.:* Claude Autant-Lara.

1933

WHAT! NO BEER? 7 reels. *Dir.:* Ed Sedgwick. *Scen.:* Carey Wilson, from an idea by R. E. Hopkins. *Dial.:* Cluett. *Photog.:* Harold Wenstrom. *Players:* B. Keaton, Jimmy Durante, Phyllis Barry, John Miljan, Edward Brophy.

PARAMOUNT — NERO FILM

1934

LE ROI DES CHAMPS-ÉLYSÉES. *Dir.:* Max Nosseck. *Scen.:* Arnold Lipp. *Dial.:* Yves Mirande. *Players:* B. Keaton, Colette

Darfeuil, Paulette Dubost, Jacques Dumesnil, Lucien Gallamand, Madeleine Guitty.

BRITISH AND CONTINENTAL FILMS *(In England)*

THE INVADERS (Full length film).

PRODUCTION RED STAR FARMAN
THE GOLD GHOST. *Dir.:* Charles Lamont. *Scen.:* Ernest Pagano and Louis Adamson. *Photog.:* Dwight Warden. *Players:* B. Keaton, Gaston Dumay, Dorothy Sebastian, Helen Feht, Harris Myers, J. Goulven, The Flying Escalanters.

EDUCATIONAL — STAR COMEDY SPECIAL. *Dir.:* Charles Lamont.

1935

ALLEZ OOP *(Scen.:* Ernest Pagano, Ewart Adamson). — **THE SERENADE.** — **THE GOLD GHOST** *(Scen.:* Ewart Adamson, Nick Barrows). — **PALOOKA FROM PADUCAH** *(Scen.:* Glenn Lambert) — **HAYSEED ROMANCE.** *(Scen.:* Charles Lamont). — **STARS AND STRIPES.** *(Scen.:* C. Lamont, E. Adamson). — **THE E FLAT MAN.** *(Scen.:* G. Lambert) — **ONE RUN ELMER** *(Scen.:* G. Lambert).

MACK SENNETT COMEDIES

1936

THE TIMID YOUNG MAN. *Dir.:* Mack Sennett.
CHRISTIE COMEDIES — STAR COMEDY SPECIAL
Short films. *Dir.:* Ray Kane. *Scen.:* Paul G. Smith — for all films,

except when indicated to the contrary.
THREE ON A LIMB — GRAND SLAM OPERA *(Scen.:* B. Keaton) **— BLUE BLAZES — MIXED MAGIC — THE CHEMIST** *(Scen.:* David Freeman).

1937

DITTO. *Prod.:* Educational Film Corp of America. *Dir.:* C. Lamont **— JAIL BAIT — LOVE NEST ON WHEELS.**

COLUMBIA

1939

MOOCHING THROUGH GEORGIA. *Dir.:* Jules White. *Scen.:* Clyde Bruckman. **— PEST FROM THE WEST.** *Dir.:* Del Lord. *Scen.:* Idem. **— NOTHING BUT PLEASURE.** *Dir.:* J. White *scen.:* Idem.

R.K.O.

1940

THE VILLAIN STILL PURSUED HER. *Dir.:* Eddie Cline.

COLUMBIA
All the following directed by Jules White, except the last.
PARDON MY BERTH MARKS *(Scen.:* Clyde Bruckman) **— THE SPOOK SPEAKS** *(Scen.:* C. Bruckman and Ewart Adamson). **— THE TAMING OF THE SNOOD** (idem).

1941

HIS EX MARKS THE SPOT *(Scen.:* Felix Adler). — GENERAL NUISANCE *(Scen.:* F. Adler and C. Bruckman). — SHE'S OIL MINE (idem). — SO YOU WON'T SQUAWK. *Dir.:* Del Lord. *Scen.:* Elwood Ullman.

1946

In Mexico: EL MODERNO BARBA AZUL. *Dir.:* Jaime Salvador (Full length film)

1952

In France: UN DUEL A MORT. (Short film directed by Pierre Blondy, from a sketch performed by Keaton at the Cirque Médrano).

1953

In Italy: L'INCANTEVOLE NEMICA. *Dir:* Claudio Gora. *Players:* Robert Lamoureux, Raymond Bussières.

APPEARANCES IN OTHER FILMS

1936 THREE MEN ON A HORSE. *Prod.:* Warner Brothers. *Dir.:* Mervyn Le Roy.

1939 HOLLYWOOD CAVALCADE (Sketch by Mal St. Clair). — THE JONES FAMILY IN HOLLYWOOD (Story by Keaton and Hoffman) — THE JONES FAMILY IN QUICK MILLIONS (idem).

1940 L'IL ABNER. *Prod.:* R.K.O. *Dir.:* Albert S. Rogell.

1943 **FOREVER AND A DAY.** *Prod.:* R.K.O. *Dir.:* René Clair, Edmund Goulding, Cedric Hardwicke.

1944 **SAN DIEGO I LOVE YOU.** *Prod.:* Universal. *Dir.:* Reginald le Borg.

1954 **THAT NIGHT WITH YOU.** *Prod.:* Universal. *Dir.:* William A. Seiter. — **THAT'S THE SPIRIT.** *Prod.:* Universal. *Dir.:* C. Lamont.

1946 **GOD'S COUNTRY.** *Dir.:* Robert Tansey.

1949 **IN THE GOOD OLD SUMMERTIME** *(Dir.:* Robert Z. Leonard). — **THE LOVEABLE CHEAT** *(Dir.:* Richard Oswald, from a story by Balzac). — **YOU'RE MY EVERYTHING.** *Prod.:* Fox. *Dir.:* Walter Lang.

1950 **SUNSET BOULEVARD.** *Dir.:* Billy Wilder.

1952 **LIMELIGHT:** *Dir.:.* Charles Chaplin.

1956 **AROUND THE WORLD IN 80 DAYS.** *Dir.:* Michael Anderson.

1960 **THE ADVENTURES OF HUCKLEBERRY FINN.** *Dir.:* Michael Curtiz.

1962 **TEN GIRLS AGO.** (Shot in Canada with Bert Lahr and Eddie Foy).

1963 **IT'S A MAD, MAD, MAD, MAD WORLD.** *Prod. and Dir.:* Stanley Kramer. — **THE TRIUMPH OF LESTER SNAPWELL.** *Dir.:* James Cahoun.

1965 **THE RAILRODDER.** *Dir.:* Gerald Potterton. — **FILM.** *Dir.:* Alan Schneider. — **PAJAMA PARTY.** *Dir.:* Don Weis. — **BEACH BLANKET BINGO.** *Dir.:* William Asher. — **DUE MARINES E UNO GENERALE.** *Dir.:* Luigi Scattini.

1966 **A FUNNY THING HAPPENED ON THE WAY TO THE FORUM.** *Dir.:* Richard Lester. — **THE SCRIBE.** *Dir.:* John Sebert.

Directed only:

1938 **LIFE IN SOMETOWN U.S.A., HOLLYWOOD HANDI-CAP, STREAMLINED SWING.**

Gag Contribution:

1944 **BATHING BEAUTY.**
1949 **A SOUTHERN YANKEE, NEPTUNE'S DAUGHTER.**

Films on Buster Keaton:

1957 **THE BUSTER KEATON STORY.** *Dir.:* Sidney Sheldon. *Scen.:* S. Sheldon and Robert Smith. *Photog.:* Loyal Griggs. *Music:* Victor Young. *"Technical Adviser":* Buster Keaton. *Players:* Donald O'Connor, Ann Blyth, Rhonda Fleming, Peter Lorre, Larry Keating, Jackie Coogan. *Prod.:* Paramount. *Distributor:* Paramount.
1965 **KEATON RIDES AGAIN.** *Dir.:* John Spotton.